And God Looked Away

(A Katrina Journal)

By:

M. Bevis

Photos by:

Katya Becnel

Entire contents © 2007

Michael C. Bevis Jr.

All photos © 2007

Katya Becnel/Phantom Photography

Printed by permission.

No part of this book may be reprinted without express, written consent from the author.

ISBN# 978-0-6151-6370-3

Design: M. Bevis/H. Post

Photo Layout & Design: M. Bevis/K. Becnel

Editing on Chap. 1-6, & "This Is For The City That Care Forgot" – Sharon Chester

All other editing by M. Bevis/H. Post

Formatting: H. Post

Printing: Lulu.com

PLEASE VISIT ON THE WEB:

http://www.myspace.com/starofkaos

http://www.paranoizenola.com

GRATITUDE

The following individuals and families made this entire adventure easier:

Jackson Troutt, Glenn Wilson, Gillian Barlow, James Wilson, MatJames Bower, Angela Franklin for being so kind to my nephews in our time of need, Jim Monaghan Jr. & the staff at Molly's at the Market, Big Jay, Shaun & Tina, Josh, Bob Edes, Paddy O' Furniture, Critter, Jim, Petey, the staff at Harry's Bar & Tables in Kansas City, Mo., Bobby Bergeron, Jordan Nash, & Nick from Calihardcore.com for the initial encouragement, and Blake Russell for putting us up in K.C. and for helping me with getting this journal started.

A special thanks to Klaus Marre, Kirsten Heintz, and Kelly & Trevva for helping us escape from the madness, and reunite with our families. Words could never express our gratitude.

Homespun smiles go to my families: Bevis, Jacobs, and Bennett – for surviving, caring, and for just being my family. And much love also to the Becnel and Chauvin families, for worrying about us, feeding and housing us, and for surviving the storm in their own right. Gratitude goes to the Pizzolato family, for the use of their boat house in False River. Thanks to the Grow family for their hospitality, and for selling us the car that got us on our way.

And a huge hug to Katya's aunt, Denise King, for helping to make our travels a reality; without her, half of this book would be an altogether different story.

Thanks to Sharon Chester for her help in editing the first half of this journal, and for her valuable advice. Same goes for Heidi Post, my formatting Samurai. You wouldn't be holding this right now if they hadn't lent me their time and expertise.

This journal is dedicated to the city of New Orleans and the people who call it home; whether they have returned or not.

It is dedicated to my family and friends, who have all suffered in varying degrees as a result of Hurricane Katrina.

It is dedicated to the memory of Glenn Marshall Rambo—the only soul I personally knew that was claimed by the storm. NOLA misses him dearly.

It is dedicated to the memory of the others that did not survive, both people and pets, whether taken by the storm or the aftermath.

It is dedicated to Katya Becnel, for watching my back before, during, and since the aftermath.

It is dedicated to you, dear viewer—for reading, supporting and caring.

INTRODUCTION

It has been more than a year since I typed up the events described herein, but in some ways you would never know it. In all honesty, the effects of Hurricane Katrina are still extremely prevalent and far-reaching, making progress halting in the least. To go into any brief descriptions or to try and encapsulate what happened in the late summer of 2005 to the Gulf Coast region of the United States of America would seem redundant -- We all know what happened, and the pages that follow are testament enough to the events that transpired in those horribly blistering days and nights, so there's no need to find yet another clever way to explain them. I'll let my journal tell the tale, and save this for an introduction that, to me, rings just a little more true to the idea behind this document. Hopefully this will serve as a basic explanation, in the broadest possible terms, of the overall feeling that I had, and continue to have about the trials and tribulations that New Orleans and the surrounding region have suffered.

When I realized that Hurricane Katrina was actually going to hit New Orleans, I somehow knew that this would be something that needed to be recorded. Being that at the time I had no way of committing what I would see and do to film or audio, the only other option was to journal, sometimes at scheduled intervals, as much as I possibly could. This turned out to be harder than it sounded, especially during the more dangerous days of the aftermath, when the act of carrying a cigarette could get you shaken down by anyone who had less than you at the moment. Much of the journal is written from notes, recollections, and photographs assembled during that time, and transcribed later when computer use permitted. As much as possible, I have taken care not to add my opinion, preferring instead to let the actions and circumstances of the moments depicted speak for themselves. At times, I do interject my perspective, but only for the sake of trying to give the reader a look into what I was thinking at that particular juncture. No matter what anyone who traffics in revisionism says, those WERE dangerous days and nights after the storm, ones that, even when escape was finally made, were incessantly desperate and hazardous.

What I have tried to bring to someone who reads this is not a historical document, nor some scathing polemic, but a simple account of what an average, middle-of-the-road, true NOLA local encountered in those days. Possibly to show that after you realize that the accusatory cries of race, class, and location were and are just red herrings, the same story is told by everyone who was affected by Hurricane Katrina, in some form or fashion. We ALL suffered in this, and no one has the market cornered in that respect. The only difference between any of us involved in the hurricane is dependant on how they acted before, during, and after the storm. The most amazing, mind-bending aspect of this entire adventure to me, is how one could get a solid glimpse into a person's true self, for better or regrettably, for worse. I saw instances of kindness, calming and safe, even as I witnessed acts of depravity and selfishness at the very next moment, or even at the very same time. It was quite disturbing, to see my city torn apart, not by some invading horde, but by the very people who were previously so proud to call it home. I still have nightmares of the city on fire, and the maddening juxtaposition of my childhood home burning even as it was submerged in those filthy floodwaters. The entire experience has left me personally feeling much smaller then I have ever felt, even though it has helped me become more assured and aware as well.

That brings me to the real reason behind this introduction—the title. I have been asked, more than a few times as to the bearing of such a particular nomenclature, and I have come to understand that it does bear a certain amount of elucidation. First off, I am not a religious man, and that confuses many of my closer friends, but another reason prompted this exposition, one that bothers me more and more all of the time. What I am speaking about is the idea that, if there is a God, that he/she/it would have an active hand in the events that transpired in those late August days of 2005 and beyond. Whether a God would pursue such an agenda for retribution, or to teach a lesson, is an exercise in fantasy to me. As far as my eyes and mind can see it, this was no Gods active doing; in fact I reason that it was quite the opposite. In Gnostic times, the idea of a Hell was far more ambiguous and internal than the one that John Milton and Dante' Alighieri have handed down since then. In those days before regimented superstition, Hell was the simple removal of God's love; more to the point, it was when God looked away from you, however briefly. It was when you felt truly and undeniably alone.

And that is what I am trying to say with the title of this journal—God looked away from us, for however miniscule a moment. Every single one of us felt a certain sort of disconnect from everything and everyone else both during and after the storm, and many of us still wrestle with that feeling to this day. If there is a God, one that is responsible not only for the creation, but the upkeep of all that we know and see, then in my mind, maybe the phone rang, because no God I could claim to worship would purposefully decide to lay claim to this disaster. To me, it only makes sense that we tasted that old-time religion, if nothing else, that Gnostic sense that God was busier when the cries rang out, and maybe in the end, that's the worst crime of all for a God . . .

After all is said and done, I am thankful that I had the prescience and forethought to actually journal everything that I experienced during that time and since. It has helped me to come to terms with the effects of the shock and trauma that I underwent, along with everybody else who was here as well. It has helped me to remember, to grow more prepared, and hopefully wiser about the outlook and preparation needed to withstand tragedy of such magnitude. It has helped me to become more of a human, and to try to always look behind the curtain, to get the story behind the attitudes and circumstances, and to not make a bad situation even worse. But in the end, the most important and lasting effect of this document, for me and hopefully for anyone that reads it, would be to combat the denial that true horror can elicit at times. I can only hope that the fear and loathing that I and so many of my fellow New Orleanians have suffered will not be forgotten, rewritten, or marginalized... and that if God truly did look away, at least someone was watching, and still is.

M. Bevis

2007

NOLA

"Those who cannot remember the past are condemned to repeat it."

- George Santayana, *the Life of Reason*

Chapter One

Saturday, August 27, 2005

– Entropy Revs the Engine –

I rose late, due to an all night jag of my favorite Playstation 2 game, Tekken 5, which had arrived just a week or so earlier in the mail. Thumbs hurting from busting out an ass-whipping to both computer-controlled foes and human adversaries alike, I bathed and called a taxi from United Cab Company. My driver, an unassuming Middle Eastern gentleman, started off this most inauspicious of days by asking me,

"So, are you leaving town today?"

Now, usually this question would mean a completely different host of personal neurotic musings, but I could feel that something was amiss. Something I should have seen on the news, had I not been trying to get my favorite character Bryan to Tekken Lord Mode . . . so I queried as to why he would ask such a question and he answered me as if I had been living in a cave for the past few days.

A storm was brewing, percolating, a course was set; didn't I know? (I didn't.) It was headed straight for us or so the local paper said. Its name a personal favorite of mine, but only in retrospect:

Katrina.

He pushed a fresh newsprint copy under my nose from the front seat. The headline was blaring all manner of paranoid prophecies; levees breaking, bodies floating, a city in ruins, its people in terror and devastation. I informed the driver that I was a local, and that I didn't buy into the scare mongering. I didn't want to add to the mad rush to leave my city, to perpetuate the notion that we, as New Orleanians, always lived halfway from our homes every summer during hurricane season. I explained to him that I had run from hurricane Georges, my family laughing at me when I called them from Texas, and how I sat in traffic, going a mile an hour upon our return a week or so later.

I told him more than that but, if you, dear viewer, are a local you probably know what I said. He responded that I was the last fare of his shift and that he was leaving as soon as he went home and gathered his family and belongings. He was packing them into his taxi and heading for high ground and good family-cooked food in Tennessee. We arrived at my destination, my employer Virgin Megastore New Orleans, just a few minutes later. I paid him his fare, tipping him well enough to cover a couple of gallons of gas for his presumably long ride out. As I crossed the street and his taxi grew smaller in the distance, I thought to myself that he was going to be sorry when he had to spend an entire day or so in traffic just to get back home on Tuesday, maybe Wednesday after the storm.

Upon entering my work, I went about my usual business as a Loss Prevention officer, prowling the sales floor for thieves and checking to make sure that all was well in general with the building and staff alike. Approximately two to three hours into my shift, the Operations Manager reported to work, pulling me aside since I was in charge of safety and related concerns. She wanted me to know that Katrina was, as reported, set for a dead-on collision with New Orleans. We didn't want to alarm anyone, so we kept the hurricane contingency plan to just herself, the Assistant Manager, and me. We all felt that at the time, it was as I had felt in the cab: more useless scare tactics and contra flow nightmares.

We kept the little TV/VCR combo set in the break room tuned to the local news all day. Co-workers milled in and out, some discussing the events, some just eating their lunch and going back to work. I conversed with some of them about this impending storm, how it could be as bad as the experts predicted but it could also be just another false alarm. I was wrapped in the same cocoon of denial, deaf from cries of "wolf" in the past. So many previous false alarms had rendered me the jaded local I will never be again... this went on for most of the day until the storm took a most ominous turn towards us. Then the Mayor, Ray Nagin, ordered a city-wide evacuation.

Contra flow time was here again. The phone lines lit up, employees were getting out of town and we worried how our record/lifestyle store was going to make its projected quota for the day with a skeleton crew. Fortunately for me, my shift ended as I watched the caretakers of the building start to board all of the windows with heavy sheets of plywood. I went home, glad to be done for the day; after all, it was my "Friday." I had the next day off and was happy about that—it meant I would have an extra day or so off of work. I amused myself on the walk home with the things I would do with my extra day; even if the power went out it wouldn't be that bad.

So I went home, played more Tekken 5, got loaded on whatever was there. I can't remember what there was, but it loosened my tongue enough to be glib about the impending doom lingering out in the Gulf of Mexico. I made some phone calls, just to see who was turning tail, and who was crazy enough to stay like I was. Mostly, I waited for my girlfriend Katya to return home. I was anxious to see her and plot out what we were going to do about this threat to our home and sanity.

She arrived home soon after I did; we conversed about the storm and how we had no way to leave in a realistic fashion. We owned no car, had nowhere comfortable to find lodging, and very little resources to travel with at that point. Besides, our respective families were staying; hers in their Uptown home and mine in my sisters newly bought Mandeville home. Talk about some strange luck—I had just helped them move in the day before on Friday.

My good friend James Wilson stopped by a bit later to play some video games, watch some weather updates, and plan out his possible evacuation if his family opted to leave town. It was looking bad in his opinion; he was going to leave if the forecast was still dismal when he awoke. I made it a point to remind him that hurricanes have a curious habit of altering course at the last minute, just as I had learned in my evacuation from Georges. James decided to sleep on our couch and, being that he was a frequent guest, we obliged him accordingly.

We all started getting hazy; sleep was decided upon considering the matter at hand. I drifted off into slumber thinking to myself that this would be just like all of the other hurricanes; more traffic jams, more angry evacuees, more apologies from city officials, more families laughing at one another on payphones across the state and the rest of the country. I honestly thought everything would be fine, as fine as hurricanes usually turned out regarding New Orleans.

I will never be that stupid again. Ever.

Chapter Two

Sunday, August 28, 2005

– Mr. Toad's Wild Ride –

I awoke to the revelation that my friend James had contacted his family, learning that they were leaving town to seek refuge at his grandmother's house in Shreveport, Louisiana. He was so rattled by their immediacy in evacuating that he had left at sunrise, before I had even woken up. This left Katya and me with a sneaking suspicion that we were possibly in for a rough time dealing with Katrina, which seemed to be bearing down on the Louisiana coast with urgency and fervor, as predicted. We made legions of phone calls, assessed our storm supplies, then Katya and I sat down for what would turn out to be the first of many meetings regarding our state of mind and our readiness to go this alone. We decided, after much deliberation, that our quaint little cottage-style apartment in the Marigny neighborhood of Downtown New Orleans might not withstand a category 5 storm. We phoned the landlord, as the work crews refurbishing an apartment in front of us had left all manner of construction-related detritus directly in front of our domicile. We were hoping that someone might come and relieve us of the duty of clearing such obviously damaging implements from our immediate vicinity. Such was not the case, so we set about the multitude of tasks at hand:

Clearing the patio of potential windblown projectiles left by errant workers.

Raising all of the books, CD's, electronics, rugs, and various valuable items out of the possible floodwater reach.

Contacting family once more, to see what the immediate future held for their safety planning.

Gathering the supplies not in evidence in our home from the local corner store.

I decided to walk down to the Frenchmen Deli to do just that. We had to stock up on some small items and I wanted to get a read on the neighborhood. My short walk told me that these were, for all appearances, the usual storm preparations. The entire neighborhood was becoming boarded up, storm-front, crack house like -- a ghost town in slow motion. As I left the deli, an old friend of mine, named Ramon, was leaving his father's vehicle to pick up his portfolios from the tattoo shop where he slung ink. The sign in the window said something about there being no more customers accepted for the day due to the oncoming deluge. He is one of the most no-nonsense, tough-as-nails men I have ever met, so I was curious as to his take on the situation. His reply was that of concern, yet not one of fear. I wished him well, he did the same for me, and then I made my way up the block back to my home. I arrived to find that a friendly neighbor was helping Katya finalize the removal of the sawhorses and carpentry supplies that littered our patio, leaving me to dummy-check our supplies inside.

I received few phone calls during that time, although a particularly memorable one was from my good friend Jackson. He offered his car, his family home in the Memphis area, his unbounded care for our safe passage out of the path of Katrina. We said no; we were going to ride it out. We would see him back home in a few days if we weren't washed out into the Gulf of Mexico, I sarcastically told him. He wished us luck and then hung up to begin his Northward trek to safer ground. I resumed our preparations, raised more items above flood level, and packed the gear we would need should the worst come to pass:

Safety candles. Battery-powered clock/radio and batteries of various types. Boxes of matches. The $1.99 flashlight I had bought just a few days before. Scissors. Two Gerber knives. Cameras and film. Multiple packs of cigarettes. My Leatherman all-purpose tool. Deodorant. Incense. Bottled water. Food, both canned and dried. Cat food, litter and a litter box. Our clothing and some washing detergent. A small silver statue of the Hindu deity Ganesh, remover of obstacles. My journal and my favorite writing pens.

After a bit, my sister called and informed me that my grandparents, who resided in the Lakeview area of town, would probably already be waiting for me when I arrived at my mother's home. This made the situation even more immediate -- I knew that if they were vacating their home, in any fashion, this was serious business. I finished out my itinerary by logging on to my MySpace website and posting a bulletin about how everyone knew I was crazy, so they shouldn't be amazed upon hearing the news that I was riding out the storm. I tempted fate by responding to emails saying that I was going to blare loud music, drink whiskey, and watch it all go down from my mother's French Quarter abode which had weathered many a storm in its century of existence. I angered the gods by cursing Poseidon and Leviathan, assuring the path I didn't know was already set before Katya and me. I called my family one more time after logging off of my PC, telling them I was staying in the city; I told them I was going to be fine. Katya's mother arrived with her car just in time to help us ferry our two cats, Jack and Loki, along with our bags of supplies, bottles of water, and hampers of clothes to our refuge.

We boarded our windows with bits of leftover wood from the aforementioned construction scrap, then we hopped in the car and rode into the heart of the French Quarter to buy the ticket and take the ride.

We arrived at my mother's apartment to find it empty and damp. The first stirrings of hurricane feeder-bands were already evident. The sky had darkened to a bruise of blues, grays and ominous in-betweens. We unpacked the supplies, loosed the cats from their carrier and awaited the arrival of my grandparents. We occupied our time by watching the news forecast doom and gloom; all entropy, all the time. Updates at every 8 of the hour. It started to dawn on me that this might actually be the one we had all feared, the big one. The storm to end all storms, at least where the Gulf Coast region was concerned... then we waited for my grandparents some more. But no one ever came. No one called.

So, while the phone was still working, I thought I would call my family to see what the holdup was about. I learned that while we were clearing the refuse from our patio, several desperate phone calls were made to coerce us out of our home and into the waiting arms of my family who had converged in totality in the Mandeville area. My grandparents were on their way there; my mother was already settling in. We were the only ones left in the city of New Orleans and the answering machine messages that we heard were just as mocking as the ones I heard during Georges, only these were concerned. This time, the laughter was gone, replaced with admonitions that suggested they thought we were out of our minds. This time, they knew the fear; it was we who were to mock them with our indifference instead of laughter. Regardless, the course was set, the barriers locked down; they had gotten out with nary a minute to spare. They were safe, or so they thought at the time. So that was it, just Katya and I, riding it out, engines be damned.

All of the meteorological experts agreed that this was the storm we had always dreaded, that the city was going to be inundated, property leveled and submerged. There would be scores of dead, threats of disease and rooftop incarceration. The city would never be the same they said, and somehow, I maintained an unhealthy amount of denial and skepticism. It wasn't until my mother called me around 8:00 p.m. that I came to find out that the only person prescient enough in my family to see the true danger had left the state altogether. My sister, wise soul that she is, had taken my two nephews, her sons, out of harm's way to the upper reaches of Louisiana, if not all the way to Texas. I called her, but she rebuffed me, out of desperation at lack of lodging and frustration for her brother who she thought was being careless and brash. It was at this point that all communication ceased, not out of downed lines, but out of the dread rearing its flowering mane at us all. We hunkered down, waited for the inevitable, for better or worse.

Sunday, 10:01 p.m.

The wind is starting up, as it is always wont to do in these things. Too early to tell if this is the real deal, we'll find out soon enough. Feelings of being lulled into a potential sense of false safety, complacency. The beast, she is on the wing, breathing hard and baring teeth. Salivation. Storm surges, on the shoreline, on the television, on our necks . . . violent pounding of precious historic treasures, relics swooning under Katrina's sway. The end is nigh, the prophets opine. HOW NIGH is the only logical response. Waiting for the inevitable seems pointless; we do it regardless. There really is no choice anyway. The roads are blocked, all egress halted. Locked in and strapped down, waiting for the mistress to arrive in grand fashion and with furious clamor, wearing her dominant best. Television transmits to me, while still functioning, that the unfortunates in the shelters are well fed but dirty even as of yet. The Superdome, home to the most famous of losers, becomes home to a new cadre of lost souls and refugees. An orgy of the damned, unable to leave, unable to behave, unwilling to try to find a light in the emergency darkness. Worries about hot dogs from the past. They are scared. Goddamn right, they should be. Maybe I should be scared too. Hide in the bathroom, in the doorframe, the wind is picking up. Katrina = the bitch goddess who came to the party late, drunk, and entirely too damn loud.

Monday, 12:17 a.m.

And yet still; more rain, more wind, more fear. More, more, more and faster. Harder. Deeper. Shop signs and hanging plants floating sideways, surreal. Bevolo lamps and unlocked windows, homes and vehicles abandoned are becoming dangerous adversaries. Just as the experts predicted, we are all truly fucked. The clouds, full and gray, are speeding across southeastern skies, either heading towards their next conquest or running from their previous crimes . . . who knows what damage has been wrought on the hinterlands? I have the fear now, but it is too late to move forward, no turning back. Airborne threats become evident, foundations and trees groan under the squall.

Monday, 2:11 a.m.

The tension proceeds apace, no option but to see this through to the final destination. The rain and storming gusts are not even close to their full force yet. They will be, they will be. The storm has just begun to touch the inner thigh of the shoreline; feeder bands flicking waterfront camps aside like so much driftwood, so many matchstick men. Can't believe people rode it out in Grand Isle, Plaquemines, or St. Bernard. They are tempting fate; she is a cruel taskmaster. The locks on the levees will be blown if the worst occurs. Don't they know their history? Whether legend or rumor or otherwise, the results will be the same as before. I hope I am wrong, but I suspect I already am on a totally opposite and maddening level. The experts are on T.V. again, vividly illustrating a striding swath of death. But then, as far as they are concerned, we are all dead anyway. This is only the beginning of the long bad time. T.V. stations, with their ready-made graphics and nonstop zeal, reprimand those of us who have chosen to take Mr. Toad's Wild Ride. We are witness to Mother Nature uncoiling, fanning plumage against the roar of jet engines and hematoma sky backdrop. An infrared Cyclops appears on the screen, wobbling and stuttering on an endless repeated loop. Except for the fact that Katrina just keeps getting closer.

Monday, 4:02 a.m.

Batten down the hatches, the rain is showing signs of intelligence. Serpentine sheets, glistening and alive it would seem, are marching in formation. Choking storm drains, battering home fronts, scaring the locals, and deafening the reporters. The surges, they recede and reappear with feather touch; hair-trigger pulled, get out the fucking way. Too late, too late. All signals fading, only the power is next. Then it's just the beast and New Orleans, along with the other poor souls who have chosen to ride it. The pulse of the city is slowly fading; lights and all the rest going out one by one . . . .

Soon we will be truly on our own.

I slept for a bit during this time, aided by a massive amount of alcohol and prescription Xanax and Hydrocodone. When the noise became too much for even that chemical cocktail to keep me down, I knew the hurricane was at full force. Katya was amazed that I could slumber during this time, but my mother always said I slept like a corpse. I hoped her colorful description didn't turn out to be dire premonition. I continued to document the storm as it happened, standing in my mother's apartment doorway, watching the chaos unfold before me. I was enraptured and afraid in equal measures. . . .

Monday, 9:42 a.m.

The Goddess, she hates us. She has been beating us all morning with no sign of relief; we are all bad little children under her gaze. The buildings surrounding our huddled sanctuary are subtracting, bit by bit, piece by piece, along with our sanity and well-being. No power now, no phone, no way out, or any hope it would seem. The worst-case scenario coming to pass. Everything is shuddering, including our fortifications; plywood trying its best to fulfill its given task. I can hear the lion's roar outside; it is hungry and screams to be fed fresh sacrifices. The water is slowly rising at the edges, so the fear ratchets up, up, up. Notch by notch, step by step, slowly it turns. . . .

The sound is as if some ancient demon has been conjured, blustering and berating this city of ghosts.

Monday, 11:21 a.m.

Flying glass, flying metal. Watch the sidewalks, don't go out of doors. Massive trauma is unavoidable for the foolhardy. Katrina rages then rests. Winds come from multiple directions, defying the experts, worrying the uninitiated. I wonder if the tourists, trapped in their suites, are regretting their holiday to the "party" city yet. The rain is traveling sideways, birds in futile quest for flight moving backwards in slow motion. One moment is calm; the next is as if Poseidon was blowing us out, over and over. Like a trick candle placed on a rotten birthday cake, dead spider placed squarely in the center. The joke is on us. Ha fucking Ha. The pressure is rising, and then falling; you can feel it in your ears. Put fresh batteries in the radio...

DO NOT DRINK THE WATER IN JEFFERSON PARISH! OR ANYWHERE ELSE FOR THAT MATTER!

PLAQUEMINES PARISH HAS BEEN RECLAIMED BY THE GULF!

CARRY A HATCHET INTO YOUR ATTIC!

PEOPLE ARE TRAPPED ON THEIR ROOFS!

PRAY TO WHATEVER GOD YOU WORSHIP FOR SAFE PASSAGE AND SPEEDY DELIVERANCE!

HIDE IN YOUR BATHROOMS, TUBS FULL OF CLEAN WATER!

The eye has passed; the threat is over. We are safe . . . for now.

Monday, 12:01 p.m. –

A CNN news van just pulled up in front of the apartment. They want to get out of the rain. That is the least of their worries. They say they want to interview us. We oblige, only after we warn them that airborne debris is a continuing threat. Our fifteen minutes of fame is at hand.

Unfortunately, so was the beginning of the aftermath.

Chapter Three

Monday, August 29, 2005

– Our Monday of Denial –

After the CNN news crew entered our command center, they immediately took to their task of interviewing us as if we were just plain fucking nuts. They were nice, but only in a patronizing way that suggested that we were, after all, just a story sidebar. They seemed to take us as a couple of crazy locals who decided to test their mettle and tempt fate. We took them into my mother's kitchen where part of the ceiling had caved in; the only apparent damage that the house had taken during the storm. We answered their queries, the whys and wherefores of the reasoning it took to make such an outwardly foolhardy decision. Then they went to the neighbor's apartment upstairs to see why the hell *they* would do the same foolish thing. And then, as quickly as they had appeared, they were gone, back from whence they came. Back to somewhere with decent food, clean water, and air conditioning. You could tell by their harried expressions that they had no idea what to expect, as the storm was still unpredictable, still squalling and thrashing in its death throes. We noticed a foreshadowing of the carnage and looting to come when we saw two Goth kids in a battered SUV pull up at the corner and take some of the broken and shattered swing lamps that had divested themselves from the building catty-corner from ours. It had not fared well in the storm; its rooftop sheared off, gutters swinging. Broken glass and shuddering windows flapping open-shut, open-shut.

We retreated into the house, to eat a bit and await the all-clear signal on the radio. We heard the first reports coming out of the affected areas, and to be honest they didn't sound so bad at first. The Superdome, refuge to the masses without solid shelter, had its roof completely blown off, revealing gaping holes and base adhesive used to secure the once recognizable white dome. As I listened to the news reporter describe the scene I was reminded of how, as a young boy, my mother told me that the Superdome was actually a flying saucer that had landed in New Orleans and decided to stay after its crew discovered the wonder of our odd little city. Now, from what I heard, it might as well be the site of the Roswell crash of 1947. At that point, we believed that the levees were intact and showing to be strong despite the storm. By all accounts, it seemed to be bad, but not nearly as bad as the pundits on the Weather Channel had predicted. The bullet had grazed us, making us bleed. We were storm-tossed and windblown, but it looked at that point to be another close call for the proud city of New Orleans.

Around 2:00 p.m., the radio announcers came on with a bulletin saying that the storm was moving to the Northeast of our location and that we could exit our houses and survey the damage

Katrina had left in her wake. Of course there were still some heavy gusts, but as long as we kept a sharp eye out for falling masonry, we were able to get a first-hand account of the aftermath. Katya and I loaded our cameras, making a trek down Dauphine Street to go and have a look at what had happened to our apartment just down the street, to our city, and our way of life.

As we made our way down the city blocks, it appeared that there was the usual damage associated with a serious storm. There were chunks of mortar everywhere -- downed gutters, windblown trash, overturned garbage cans, and upended newspaper kiosks. There were many other people out as well, rubbernecking as we were, at the terrible beauty that Katrina had created. It wasn't until we reached the last two blocks of Dauphine Street before Esplanade Avenue that we started to understand this was quite a bit different. A well-known dog park, surrounded by iron fences and brick fortifications, was blasted wide open; trees completely uprooted and lying in the middle of the road. Down the side streets Katya snapped pictures of me walking up the trees that had fallen into houses, creating bridges to nowhere. At that point it was a wonderland of destruction . . . no immediate danger, just wide-eyed amazement at the power of Mother Nature.

When we came to Esplanade Avenue proper, the realization struck: Katrina had beaten us hard and fast. The entireties of both sides of the street were an orgy of flooded water, fallen trees blocking even foot travel. Downed power lines made even thinking about traversing that particular area impossible. Walking a few yards down, we found a safer area just about passable, so we jumped over and through the dirty water into the Marigny. Katrina had really done a job there, as some buildings were outright destroyed, crumbled security gates blown clean out of their moorings. More trees everywhere; water, water, and more water. We zigzagged through the streets leading to our home and were amazed when we found it to be completely unscathed. The area surrounding it had the feel of a carpet bombing, but our little home stood proud and intact. A tree had fallen from the neighboring yard, its topmost branch barely touching our bedroom wall. Whew. We opened the door and everything was where we had left it, the way we had left it. We grabbed some basic extras left in our previous day's rush, and then set back out to explore some more of the Godzilla-like devastation that seemed to be everywhere.

After about an hour or so of snapping photos and making sure that our respective workplaces were intact, (they were) we were amazed to see that a daiquiri shop across the street from the Virgin Megastore had been *completely destroyed* during the hurricane. Its doors, glass, and wood were in the street, leaving the bar exposed and vulnerable. We wondered how long it would take for the liquor (sitting within easy reach behind the bar) to be appropriated for an impromptu hurricane party, then began our way back to my mother's home to listen to more radio. We crossed through Jackson Square, finding it deserted and scattered with paper, trash, leaves; nary another human in sight. We tried to pass down Pirates Alley, only to find it blocked by massive oak trees that had fallen behind St. Louis Cathedral. We made our way around the block, and as we came around the corner on Royal Street, we heard some people talking. They were discussing the "Touchdown Jesus" -- a statue of Christ that was something of a landmark for many French Quarter residents; it lived in the courtyard behind the cathedral. They were using words like "miracle" and "inspiring," so we quickly walked the block to where we viewed one of the most enduring images of the entire storm.

Every tree in the courtyard behind St. Louis Cathedral had fallen. Huge oak trees, at least a century old, had fallen in perfect formation *around* the statue of the Christ. It was truly amazing, making me wonder, if only briefly, if there was actually something to all of that miracle stuff those Christians were always going on about. Again, more pictures, more gawking, more oohs and aahs. We turned and headed the block or so to my mother's house for food, rest, hot showers (the water was still on at this point), and maybe a nap. We did just that, serenaded by our little radio into fitful, sweaty slumber by stories of rooftop refugees, angry residents, horror and depravity at the Superdome. We expected this much disruption, so we were able to drift off for a little while.

I awoke around 9:00 p.m. to find Katya rustling about, feeding the cats and munching on some trail mix we would loathe after all was said and done. It was dark as pitch everywhere, so she had lit some candles and the ambiance was almost romantic, if not for the knowledge of the destruction outside. We could hear people in the streets shouting and howling in the night. The hurricane party, it seemed, had begun. Johnny White's, a longtime holdout of too many storms to count, was a block down on Bourbon Street. As usual, they were open and serving warming beers and cocktails. The bar doesn't even have locks on the doors; such is their homespun commitment to New Orleans. You could hear revelers laughing -- whistles and catcalls in the city dark. I went to the corner to assess what there was to see, as flashlight beams and candled balconies completed the serene atmosphere. If it weren't for the heat and humidity, those first moments on that night after the storm would have been Paradise. We had the city to ourselves, and, I must admit, I enjoyed the prospect of an empty city at first. We had no idea we were actually on an island, as levees had indeed broken, filling most of the surrounding area with poisonous water. I went back, grabbed my flashlight, and told Katya I was going to find a payphone. Then I headed out to explore the French Quarter and see if it was connected to the outside world. I didn't want Katya to come with me at first because I knew that there was a possibility of danger. It was best if I canvassed the area and saw what was functional, what was safe, before taking her with me into the creeping dark.

It was at this point that the entire situation became more like a movie or video game than any consensus reality. The French Quarter was *pitch black*, giving the entire proceeding a Zombie-movie quality. This effect would persist throughout the span of the situation, but on this night it was FUN, like you had extra quarters and an infinite time clock on the game. I slipped into "ninja mode" and crept along the streets of my city in the plentiful shadows. Dodging harsh epithets and walking calmly past locals just having a good time, I made my way systematically throughout the French Quarter, searching in vain for a working payphone. There was enough storm related damage to make travel halting at times. The initial stirrings of unrest had begun -- screams too urgent to be celebration, too loud to be in frivolity. After about an hour or so of trying every pay phone I could find, I decided that Katya was probably getting worried. I made my way back down Orleans Avenue, walking past Johnny White's once more. The bar was in full swing by then, candles and laughter and diehard locals too smart to be alone, too stupid to have left town.

As I passed the bar, my flashlight caught upon a pair of boots in the gutter. I shined my light on them, saying hello to whomever it might be lurking in the side street there. The boots responded with a gruff voice that I recognized with much relief and familiarity. It was an old friend, Big Jay from the Famous Door on Bourbon street, one the toughest motherfuckers to ever walk the Earth as well as a helluva good guy. He was sporting weapons and bristling with animal fervor, in his element for once in his life, and maybe just liking it. I hailed him by his name -- he seemed surprised at first, then relaxed as he recognized my lanky stance in the shifting darkness. He was sort of drunk, enough to care and not care in equally opposing directions. He told me that there were only a few places open that were serving and safe. He lived above a well-known strip club on Bourbon Street. He said he had extra rounds to fetch and maybe a bowl of weed to calm our nerves. The kicker was that the payphone across the street from his apartment, three blocks from my starting point in the beginning, worked quite well. We made our way down Bourbon Street amongst the other shell-shocked members of our city. The payphone worked and I left messages on my answering services about hunting zombies, silly and in ignorance of the events unfolding around me as I spoke. You could hear the laughter in the background as I recited my message right before I hung up. Then it was time to cross the street so Jay could grab his fortifications.

I stopped at the entrance to his abode, as Jay went inside to fetch his arsenal. I was entranced by the sounds of New Orleans gone feral, atavistic. Gunfire, auto and semi-auto, echoed from more than the ghettoes all at once, then not at all. Sounds of a party mixed with the sounds of a funeral, surreal and hard to erase. Disaster everywhere, denial even more prevalent. No matter what, we party on and on . . . the locals always do. Jay returns; no weed, but he has plenty of bullets and a flask of Vodka. He tells me that an Irish pub owned by some good people is open; so we should go see what is going on there. So we do, finding warm beer, gutter punks, and displaced gay men, whose disco bars are closed, singing songs only gay men would find appropriate. Dogs. Tattoos and piercings, some weirdoes streaking into the night because they finally can. A human circus in the literal sense was at work there on the first night. We felt at ease, had a beer, a couple of shots, and discussed what we thought was going to happen to the city. Everything we thought and said was wrong, wrong, wrong.

Eventually, my thoughts turned to Katya and how she must be getting *really* worried by then. So I told Jay I would be back, and set out for my mother's place to tell Katya about our little reality show without the cameras and the stay-at-home audience. When I arrived, she was peevish; calming down only when I assured her that the outside world beyond my mother's home was reasonably safe. We readied ourselves with weapons and pep talks and then went to explore the urban wasteland together. As we walked the semi-deserted streets, I soothed Katya by pointing out that you could actually see the Milky Way from the French Quarter, probably for the first time in 50 years. It was beautiful sharing that with her, on a balmy night when time had stopped and the rhythm was unique. We commented on the ambiance, how it reminded us of zombie movies, war movies, and curious nightmares. We returned to the bar to find it still in excelsis, and we were happy to have common brethren in evidence on such an isolated night.

After a few hours of talking to other concerned denizens, Katya, Jay, and I decided to wander around just to see what we could on that amazingly clear and interesting night. We walked to Decatur Street to hopefully get down to the Moonwalk on the Mississippi River, if it wasn't blocked off by water or police barricades. As we made the corner onto Decatur Street, we were amazed to witness a parade of Wildlife & Fisheries trucks, all hauling any manner of waterborne rescue devices, big and small. After fifteen minutes or so, they passed, and we made comments about how this must have meant that the destruction Katrina had wrought was worse than we knew even then. We made our way up to the river; you could have heard a pin drop. There were no artificial vessels of any kind; it was as if the clock had turned back 2000 years. It was the one truly quiet moment in any of what I will report and was so unsettling and creepy that we left sooner than we should have as a result. We decided that it was time for us to return to my mother's house to plan the next day, should this realize to be as bad, if not worse, than the rumors we heard on the streets.

Throughout the night, we kept hearing stories of rape, pillage, and plunder. The Superdome was reportedly an abattoir -- you only went there if death was the only alternative for sure. We had no idea that the levees had failed, but we were already calling ourselves the residents of "The Island of New Orleans." The only looting we heard of was from a few bars, their liquor supplies going faster than on St. Patrick's Day in the Irish Channel. And yeah, the gunfire . . . booming, echoing, frightening. We arrived at our command center, pouring whiskey and vodka until well past the midnight hour. My mother's place had the only light on Dauphine Street as the natural gas was still on. As we drank, we mused on the situation we were in. Some thought it was apocalyptic, some said it was utopia. Our conversation paused when we saw two ragged figures emerge from the inky beyond down Dauphine Street from the direction of Esplanade Avenue.

Two young men stumbled lazily down the street, shocked and shaken. They looked like citizens of St. Bernard Parish, reportedly one of the hardest-hit areas of town. They were. We never really found out their names, but the story they told us probably erased any trace of true reality. They had escaped from Hell they said, giving us an inkling of the horrors to come over the next two and a half days. As they settled onto the sidewalk after our salutations, we learned that they had come out of a home that had been inundated so quickly that they literally escaped with their lives and the soiled clothing on their backs. They were among the lucky; another escapee with a flatboat had seen them on their roofs and rescued them, having to glide past other victims along the way. They told us how the diesel fuel in the water scalded their extremities, peeling their skin and causing wounds. They also intimated various other tragedies unrelated to them that were like nightmares come alive and wriggling at the foot of your bed. They told us about an elderly woman, clutching her gutters in water too high for anyone, anytime. She was screaming about the gas, the gas . . . she was dying and nude.

They smoked cheap generic menthol cigarettes and thankfully took the water, crackers, and whiskey we offered them. To say that they were in shock would be an understatement in the extreme. They told us that the water in their parish was so high that they had to push the hanging traffic lights out of the way during their escape or else they would hit their heads on them. They told us of the sound of the levees breaking, the sound of water moving in too fast, too close, and too personal. They told us of the other voices screaming into the night, suddenly bringing their situation into sharp focus. We gave them as much comfort as we could; tried to guide them to safe harbor and give them some sort of advice that would ease their pain.

When they decided to leave, we asked them what their plans were -- where to from there? They responded, saying that they were going to the Superdome; they had heard buses were ferrying evacuees out of town to safer havens, showers, and clean beds. We relayed what we had heard about the Superdome, the forced sexual liaisons, the gang-beatings, the lack of food, and water; anything decent to the human soul. We warned them away, telling them to go use the pay phone I had found earlier, while wishing them the luck of the Gods. They shuffled back into the abyss from whence they had come, leaving us shaken and disturbed. After a few more cocktails and talk of apocalyptic movies and the fear of automatic handguns, we bade Jay farewell. He agreed to meet up with us the next day to work out a better plan -- one that was more defensive and survivalist in overall thought seemed to be the right choice. We were more than a little tipsy, and had to sleep it off in order to handle what was turning out to be more than just the usual storm aftermath. Katya and I slept apart due to the heat, almost nude, in my mother's sauna dwelling.

As the first echoes of the rescue helicopters puréed their way into the psyches of the New Orleans survivors, we dreamt of almost anything but the waters that had flooded our childhood homes.

Chapter Four

Tuesday, August 30, 2005

– Apocalypse Tuesday –

We had slept fitfully the night before; the choppers and the first stirrings of the fear kept us tossing and turning. That, coupled with the previous night's libations, made our second day of the aftermath difficult to start in a pleasant manner.

Since the natural gas oven at my mother's house still operated, Katya and I made some food. We ate in silence, sweat dripping off of every extremity. We listened to the radio, jaws gaping lower and wider, as the stories poured out of its tiny speaker: static and nothing but bad news. The levees had broken, not just in St. Bernard but also in Lakeview where I had grown up. It came as a major shock to the both of us that parts of Uptown were flooding. The water was reportedly rising quickly enough for the residents there to see its progress into their homes. Katya's family was Uptown, in the Broadmoor area, presumably trapped in their home. The French Quarter was completely surrounded by flooding and debris. As far as we could tell, we were the only section of town that was relatively unscathed. Then the radio came alive with stories of violence, lawlessness, and chaos. We had heard rumors of the insanity at the Superdome. Now there was some truth: naked, rank, and terrifying. Rapes, multiple rapes, molestations, and suicides. Fires. Beatings. Death, death, death. All true, all real, all sad and tragic. There were troops there, but only to keep the evacuees inside, locked in like so many prisoners. Left to fend without fresh water, food, the pleasure of a simple act like smoking a cigarette -- things were getting ugly. They were reportedly defecating anywhere, anytime, at will and without dignity or caution. People were escaping, jumping over the breezeways into the three feet of water that surrounded the structure so many people loved and had recognized as a symbol of our fair town. Then we heard something that chilled us stone cold.

There were no 911 emergency services, none at all. People were trapped on their roofs, surrounded by filthy water, diesel fuel, and corpses. The 911 operators were forced to listen to these refugees, unable to send help in return for the loss and terror on the other end of the line. Reports kept coming in; there was looting and violence in the drier parts of town, namely the French Quarter. The Police had lost all communication with one another, relegating them to the status of a gang. We heard the first rumors of snipers, armed invasions into institutions; thugs stealing generators and belongings by force. This was the first inkling of the descent into madness -- we knew right then that everything had changed drastically. We decided to make a pact, to keep each other sane and alive, never letting the other down, never being rude to anyone, no matter what they did. It was best not to invite confrontation or attention -- keep the brim of your hat turned down. We grabbed our knives and realized for the first time that we were in for the very real possibility of hurting or killing someone. The realization struck with such force, such tenacity, that we were rendered speechless for more than a moment. Sobered, we started getting dressed, and soon after there was a knock on the door.

It was Big Jay, dressed, ready, and armed to the teeth. He had seen some of the initial looting and unrest in the streets in just the three blocks' walk to our place. We drank some water, talked more plans out, and went over what was possible, what was not. Jay and I decided to go down to the phone on Bourbon Street to make some calls, leave messages on my machine. Messages that would let people know I was alive, although the situation was not getting better. Along the way we saw packs of kids, roaming about, prying doors and windows; they were looking for anything to steal. Jay had made his way down to Razoo bar, scoring packs of precious cigarettes for Katya and me. We could see that one of the myriad T-shirt shops down the street was falling prey to a group of roughly five or so kids. They were indiscriminately pulling shirts out through the window.

An NOPD police cruiser, its body punctured by a hail of bullets, and all its windows bashed in or shot out, came rolling down Bourbon Street the wrong way. Inside the car I could see officers brandishing exotic weaponry: Mac-10, Mp5, Uzi, Tec-9, and Glock. On the hood and trunk of the car was an officer apiece. One of the officers was brandishing an AK-47 assault rifle, and the other a 12 gauge shotgun. They looked tired, yet resolute, albeit maddened by their unraveling city. We alerted them to the completely pointless looting going on just down the block, and they sped off to deal with their newest concern. We quickly walked the other way, preferring to stay far away from any confrontations. We arrived back at my mother's just as Katya was walking out of the bathroom, dressed and ready. After letting her know that the streets were indeed slipping into chaos, the three of us sat down and hashed out what resources we had in our favor.

Katya and I decided to go back to our apartment to looter-proof our most precious possessions one last time, and to grab some other needed items. Jay told us that he was returning to the bar we had been at the night before. He told us that they were going to garrison the street, lock down for the perceived war on the horizon. We made plans to meet him there, to hopefully hang out amongst other like-minded locals. It seemed like the perfect plan -- hang around the bar until night fell, drink a little but not too much, get to know some new people, maybe even make new friends. They had Jay's approval and I knew a couple of other cool cats, Keith and Dan, who would also be there. We hit the street with a cautious awareness and newfound understanding of our predicament.

As we walked back to our home in the Marigny, the day was oppressively hot and humid. Not a cloud in the sky, although there were plenty of helicopters. We arrived home, finding no evidence of any attempt at a forced entry. We grabbed important documents, more knives, and a few other foodstuffs not perished in those two days since the power had gone out. Then we hid all of our most precious items, just in case a violation occurred to our simple little home. We left, not looking back, hoping for the best, and yet preparing for the worst. We set out down Frenchmen Street to see if the looting had started there as well. There was no one else on the street so we walked right down the center of Frenchmen. Katya alternated between walking her bike, and occasionally riding it. We walked up to the Apple Barrel, a tiny local bar, to find an elderly black gentleman sitting on a dilapidated bench outside. His lap was full of water, cookies, fruit, and cigarettes. We stopped to ask him if he was okay, and if he needed anything. He replied that he was from the assisted living community building around the corner, and that he was fine; he just didn't want to be in there all day. He liked sitting on that bench and that was just what he was going to do, damnit. He offered us water and fruit which we warmly received. He even offered me cigarettes but I declined as I had packs at home. We made some chit-chat about the insanity and tragedy growing up around us, then bid him farewell. We had to check on our workplaces, to make sure they hadn't fallen prey to the shopping-spree that seemed to be happening everywhere.

As we wandered back into the French Quarter proper, you could tell that some of the damage you saw was not storm generated. We reached the end of Decatur Street and there was definite evidence that the looting had been going on. Storefront windows were broken inward; deep slash marks on cars that suggested intrusion by crowbar. Some of the stores attacked by looters were obvious choices: food stores, restaurants with good liquor and stocked freezers. Some of the shops picked clean were seemingly done so out of greed: clothing stores, retail outlets, and the like. We went to Katya's workplace to find that there was plenty of fresh water there, delivered sometime just before Katrina had struck. This made the situation tolerable, as we had not stocked up on enough fresh water before the storm. We left the water there, heading out for the Virgin Megastore down the street. Virgin was still untouched, pristine amongst the pilfering and destruction. As we were leaving, we noticed that the Walgreen's pharmacy just across the street had been looted. We decided against going in, for fear that the Police who were roving about might decide to actually arrest us, or possibly do something even worse to us. It was decided that we would return to the command center, pack supplies for our rendezvous, and gird ourselves for the night to come.

We did just that, gathering food and weapons, a couple of bottles of liquor, flashlights, and water. We didn't want the kids at the bar to think that we wanted anything but companionship, refuge, and good freakish vibes. We brought everything we would need that night, mostly out of survival instinct, but also so that no one would get the wrong idea about us. It was better to avoid giving the impression that we were there to drink all their hooch and not share what we had. We thought that even though we would know only three of the people there, like minds would prevail. Katya and I sincerely felt that this was the right place to go, and as we hit the street, we were curious as to what the night held in store for us.

At first, our arrival at the bar was uneventful. We inquired as to Jay's whereabouts; he boisterously emerged from one of the darker corners of the bar. He told us to chill, hang out, and get comfortable. We picked a seat on some steps across the street from the bar and settled in to watch the crew prepare to barricade the street. We didn't have long to wait. They started by hauling the mailboxes, newspaper kiosks, scrap metal, and windblown trash that were scattered everywhere. As they attempted to block traffic from both ends of the block, I could tell the other residents on the street were not enamored with this decision. You could hear their distrust; who were these brash young white boys who owned that bar, and now apparently the whole damn street? The mob did not care; they just continued dragging waste from other parts of the streets onto their roadblock. They missed only one thing during that time: as they were securing their people from perceived threats, they were also sealing themselves off from courtesy and common sense. We sat there for an hour, give or take. I made one entry into my forgotten journal, and it fits the tone of their scared and paranoid dispositions.

Tuesday, 5:00 p.m.

Total and complete chaos; everywhere. The city is an island, impenetrable and resolute. We are trapped, all of us -- together. Knives drawn, and guns at the ready, literally. At night, the city festers, too much opportunity; too little logical thought. Blasted mortar, broken dreams, and hope and cares. This is the moment when the resolve of the common man or woman is tested. Martial law and rising water. Not enough sleep and nowhere near enough food. The freaks are at the ready though, brandishing weapons and disgusting snarls. Their dogs are fighting; they think it is wrong. They are alone amongst their crowd. They might as well go to the Superdome. They would fit right in there, square peg in square hole. I have a bad feeling about this.

I hailed Dan, one of the people there that I did know, and he responded with his usual smile and joking demeanor. He provided Katya and me with a sense of safety, just by treating us with kindness. We owe him more than we could ever give for his display of class and grace. Then we saw Keith, another friendly face; he brought us smiles, and drank from the bottle of scotch I had brought as a contribution of goodwill and pre-emptive payback. Big Jay sat with us for a bit, talked about his worries, and then went to help gather supplies and ammo. These would be the only pleasant interactions we would enjoy with the people assembled there on that searing August afternoon.

As for the other members of the group, I have no favor towards any of them. They were sullen, snobbish, cliqued, and rude. They rebuffed our attempts at basic conversation, even snarling at Katya and me when we offered to share our meager supplies. They were pulling the pack mentality, which could have been a good thing, only they were becoming isolated and scary as hell to be around. It stung to feel so disregarded, so treated like tourists when we were locals, when these people weren't even really from New Orleans . . . well, maybe a few, but that is beside the point. They displayed their ineptitude on a massive level when they took a "family" portrait, their ranks closing file, masks and guns and stupidity and braggadocio colliding in wide paths. Worse yet, one dreadlocked cunt didn't even realize that she was pointing her pistol directly at Katya and me the whole time. Or maybe she did -- either way, it was a telling indictment of the stupidity we were surrounded by. We quickly realized what we were faced with: an asinine, hapless, scared, and under-experienced bunch of movie-tough children.

It became all too clear how large a group of assholes we were consorting with when a simple rumor became reality to the entire tribe. Someone proclaimed to the unwashed mass that the National Guard was in town abducting people at gunpoint, conducting forced evacuations. I thought, surely these wise street traveled souls would know bullshit when they smelled it. Surely they wouldn't turn tail and hide from such obvious trifle. Not so, and as they scurried, I asked Jay what their plan was; the fear was at a screaming pitch. He said to wait a moment; a plan was in action. Moments later, everyone started moving to another building down the block. They had rented a room somewhere, and were relocating there to hide from the phantom guard. I asked Jay if he thought that the forced evacuations were a reality. I started to tell him that I wasn't so sure about the rumor, being that I know more than a bit about the legality of said acts. Right about then, the owner of the bar walked up, flustered and suspicious. He was eyeing my bottle of scotch as if it was stolen from his shithole bar, then eyeing me, and eyeing Katya. He started asking me what I was talking about with Jay. I asked him if he thought that the forced evacuation was possible, how he thought the guard could legally do that to people, to which he cockily replied, with obvious disdain for the both of us:

"I don't know, but I just hope you have somewhere to go. Why don't you just come see us tomorrow, okay?"

I told that simple dive bar owner that everything was cool, swallowed my pride, and shelved the desire to shut that cunt up for good. I was mostly intent on protecting Katya from drama and violence, as well as myself, to be honest. I handed Jay the bottle of scotch, as way of saying "FUCK YOU" and we got the hell out of that legion of shit necks. Aside from Dan, Keith, and Big Jay, the rest of that group squandered what could have been a good moment in our ruined city. Their inhospitable attitudes only made it worse for themselves and anyone around them.

Katya and I, we're true New Orleans locals. We treated everyone with kindness, support, and trust in an untrustworthy predicament. All these sad little children sped was inclusion, suspicion, and scorn. You could see how they loved giving the local women of color batteries; it made them look good. But the idea of being kind to freaks of their own stripe, true locals asking for nothing other than companionship, they shunned outright. We were saddened; we had geared up for a meeting of the minds, and possible salvation in the form of fellow eccentrics. This was a first lesson in how the storm had taken people and indulged their base psyches, taking good people and reducing them to shadows of their former selves. All one had to do was look around, hour after hour; people were reaching their breaking point. To see it in familiar faces was painful, and it reinforced something very important: Katya and I knew immediately that we were respectively the only person the other could trust. The implications of that knowledge sank in as we made our way back to my mother's dank and lonely sweatbox.

Arriving at the house just after sundown, we listened to the radio, and talked to the neighbors who had also ridden out the storm. They were optimistic because the water was on, and so was the gas, so all could be okay despite the flood waters. One of the neighbors, Jim, who occupied a slave quarter apartment upstairs, seemed ready to take on the world. He told us he had all the crackers, peanut butter, rolling tobacco, and rainwater he needed. He said that he was a French Legionnaire, and I really thought he believed it. We listened to the radio some more -- random tales of insanity and sub-humanism. Stories of drowning, bodies floating, brutal beatings and multiple stabbings. A family held hostage in Westwego by gun toting maniacs who ate their food rations and drank their water supply. This all happened while the family was tied up and abused. Someone somehow got through to the Fire Department and told them that the house was on fire, knowing that was the only reason someone might respond. The flood waters had started to level out, the reporters said, and in the dark we imagined many nightmarish scenarios of lawlessness and chaos beyond the dry paths of the Quarter.

Worst of all, neither of us knew anything about our families' whereabouts or well-being, or they of us. Carrying that weight was unbearable, but there were more important things at hand, such as basic survival. We decided to barricade ourselves into my mother's house that night, to fend off unwanted intrusions -- to stay safe and alive. The end was actually nigh, the jokes were gone; the romantic movie-inspired apocalypses were trite. This was the real deal -- do or die, fight or flight. We wondered if we could hot wire a car left abandoned outside of our fort since before the storm -- no such ingenuity. We plotted and fought and planned and worried and fell into sleep amidst the screams, the helicopters, and the mounting dread that was inching closer second by second.

This was our Apocalypse Now, our moment when we asked for the person in charge . . . only to be asked if it was us.

Chapter Five

Wednesday, August 31, 2005

– Our Holiday of Insanity –

Shit . . . New Orleans.

Katya and I started in and out of sleep all night, heat and horror and hunger doing the work. The helicopters were omnipresent, chopping into the sky, sometimes two or three or four at a time. We got up around 11:00 a.m., and proceeded to eat old leftovers and drink simple water to conserve supplies. It was only after Katya used the bathroom for the first time that day that we discovered the newest and most damaging fact in the entire situation. The water supply to the entire city had been shut off. This meant we were screwed, and in a big way. No more showers, no more shitting comfortably.

Almost on cue, a loud banging at the front door scared the living daylights out of us. It was the upstairs neighbors; they were losing their minds over the lack of running water, which meant no flushable waste. They were headed out of town and told us we really were crazy if we stayed behind now. We told them that we still didn't have a car, and that there was no way into the city now that the flooding had begun; we were stuck there. They left, tires squealing, as Katya and I started to realize that most of the other people in the Quarter had started to disappear as well. It was becoming a ghost town at this point; you could hear some occasional laughter in the distance from Johnny White's which was still going strong, otherwise . . . nothing.

After changing clothes and speaking with Jim on the patio about conspiracy theories regarding water turnoff, we left our command center to explore yet more of the wasteland. As we made it to Bourbon Street, almost everyone we saw was heading for the Superdome. Fools, thought I, they must not have radios, not know what lay in wait for them. We saw a few castaways like us hanging around; they told the same stories of bravery or being stranded. We were also told that Coop's Place, a great eatery on Decatur Street was going to be handing out their unspoiled food around 2:00 p.m. that day. We smiled and started off to find working phones. We were hoping to get through to someone, anyone, before we were able to enjoy real food amongst possibly cool people. As fate would have it, even the phone across from Big Jay's place didn't work anymore. We found some phones that worked sporadically, but only enough to reach one of Katya's uncles.

Good news was, everyone survived and was planning escape at a date to be announced. This bolstered her spirits a bit, as it did mine, but there was so much to worry about that we remained stone-faced. The entire time we carried out these chores, we had knives in our hands, and at the ready. I would greet passerby with my usual,

"Are you OK? How are you doing?"

If they looked me in the eye, responded with pleasantries, I'd turn the knife down, and away from them. If they didn't, well, I'm sure you can guess what it looked like. This was the way we were until we left the city. Yes, we were scared, but we were not about to shut out anyone that was nice to us. If we had done that, we might have shut out a future friend, or possibly even a savior; maybe even someone who needed help more than we did. The phones were more pain than we could stand, stealing precious quarters, and dropping ring tones in mid-brap. A decision was made to try to go down the street to Walgreen's pharmacy, as Katya had prescriptions that were running out quickly. We had heard that the police had taken control of the store, in order to allow people to retrieve survival-only items, as an erstwhile humanitarian cause. We spoke with the officer there, his AK-47 dangling downward, slung over his shoulder. He informed us that the first people who looted the pharmacy had taken all of the drugs right off the bat. We figured as much, we told him, but could we please go see if her meds were there? Hers are for a real medical condition, not something you can get a high from. He responded that the looters had destroyed anything left; it was too hazardous to even take a look. He jokingly told us that he hoped whoever tried to smoke her medicine died, then went back to his job.

We shelved any attitude we had about that situation, preferring instead to check on my workplace just across the street. The Megastore was standing tall, and looking pretty damn good for its trouble. That done, we ambled down Decatur Street to see if the tale of good food at Coop's was indeed true. The further we traveled down Decatur, the more evident it became that the looting and destruction was worsening by the hour. You'd see other people with a crazed look in their eye, checking us out, ascertaining whether on not we looked weak or in possession of something they might risk trouble over taking from us. We were almost to Coop's when we saw that a friend's house was alive with activity, with people coming and going in and out of their gated entrance. We peeked down the alleyway to his house to find that he and his family were indeed still there. The entire complex of four apartment units had chosen to stay through the storm there -- some were trapped in the city, some just waiting for the right moment to make good their escape. There were children there, making the entire thing sad in a way, especially when you got a good look at the kids.

Their mother had scrawled on their bellies, in crude Sharpie lettering:

IF YOU FIND ME CALL MY GRANDMA AT: (phone #)

We quickly entered our friend's apartment to see what the deal was for them at that point. They had a land line phone that was still working, and that was the good news. The bad news was that the only entry or exit point in the city was the Crescent City Connection Bridge. You had to get out under your own power, any way you could. We tried more phone calls, but made little progress. Our friends were worried about the threat of flood, so we helped them move some furniture to higher ground. Then we bade them farewell, hoping to see them again soon, and in good health. We resumed our move to Coop's, moving fast and with purpose.

As we made the approach to Coop's, we noticed that Molly's at the Market was open. This was a popular bar amongst the hip underground set, so it made us feel a little at ease to see that they were at work. We spoke with Jim Monaghan Jr., the owner of Molly's; he told us that Coop's was talking about preparing the food, but with the water being out, it was not looking good. He told us there were cigarettes and beer for sale in his bar and that we were welcome as long as Molly's was open. One of Jim's friends made a joke after I thanked him for his generosity and sanity that that might be the first time anyone has said anything like that to him. I don't care. Either way, I meant it then and even more so now.

We had found an oasis. No paranoia, no bad vibes. We went into the bar, grabbed packs of smokes and lukewarm beers, and then sat down and tried to relax. The good news continued when a dear friend of mine, MatJames, came sauntering into the bar with a couple of friends of his. He looked stable, so I asked him about his story, and then told him mine up to that point. We both relaxed measurably; to be in comfortable company was just what we all needed. MatJames was telling us about the bodies he had seen, floating, rotting, and ominous. He told us our first stories about the Convention Center—it had been broken into to be used as an impromptu refuge when the Superdome became too full; too damaged. He told us of the atrocities going on there that made the Superdome seem almost tame by comparison, and warning us away from there. He had ridden all over the accessible parts of the city on his trusty bicycle, taking in all manner of simple beauty and horror; sometimes pedaling faster.

A few beers later, and we heard a commotion outside on the street. Most of the bar emptied out to see what was happening. Five police officers were pushing a man against a wall; their Mp5's and shotguns were pointed squarely at his cranium. They were telling the motherfucker to get down, down motherfucker -- NOW. We retreated into the bar and, just as suddenly as they had appeared, the cops sped off, their tires squealing. We heard another set of tires groan outside seconds later, only this time it was a truckload of people. They were screaming that the police were chasing them, firing at them, hollering that they needed to get out of there . . . then they sped away as well; more fear and loathing. We went back inside Molly's and finished our drinks, just to be safe. Another beer or so later, the party moved cautiously out to the sidewalk -- it was hot inside the bar. We sat and traded stories, of the city, or what was left of it. We cracked morbid jokes, either making those around us wince, or busting up those who knew what we were doing with our comic relief. More good souls started arriving, and for a brief moment it felt like any other day in the French Quarter. Just another day of sipping beers, making jokes, and hating the heat. We heard some of the most unbelievable rumors that afternoon:

Sharks free from the Aquarium downtown were swimming down Magazine Street. An alligator, mad and thrashing, had bitten a cop on the flooded end of Canal Street. The levees were going to burst everywhere, filling even the French Quarter with water.

These made us laugh, only because we could not believe that people would buy into such spurious conjecture. We started to feel a bit safer; it was a good moment we had stumbled upon, outside of Molly's. But then we saw more looters, running down the streets with bags full of things that no one would need after a catastrophe. The police, they were everywhere, cruising, shaking us down visually -- they didn't want us there. Yet more helicopters, flying low and successive. This went off and on for a few hours until an old friend of mine came stumbling down the street. He had a Louisville slugger in his hand, and was drunk out of his ever-loving mind. Almost falling down, he gave me a hug and let me in on a secret: He had the keys to his restaurant workplace. There was food, beer, and even cold water. He also lived in an apartment complex that was gated, had three extra empty apartments, and a swimming pool. I almost fainted when he invited Katya and me to a cookout/swimming party. This would have been welcome even if the storm had never happened; at that point it seemed like a gift from the heavens. He told us to meet him there in a couple of hours, so we resumed drinking and talking to the other locals present even after he had stumbled away. Roughly fifteen minutes later, we saw a few local kids towing baskets full of food to their homes. The word was that the cops had opened the A&P grocery near my mother's apartment and were conducting another humanitarian aid effort of their own. Katya and I made quick farewells, hoping that this wasn't just another rumor. We pretty much ran to the A&P; making lists of what we would want, should the rumors turn out to be true. When we arrived, though, there was no such luck. The police were there, but only to arrest the people that had broken into the A&P.

Damn. Another bullshit story; another set of downward, dejected stares.

Watching the police stuff some fool into their cruiser was Bob, a local thespian who also worked in the video section of the Megastore. He had heard the commotion, and ended up arriving at the same time as the pigs. After the usual salutations, we asked him what his story was in all of this. He was in the same situation as we were -- little to no supplies, no way out, and very few trusted confidants, if any. We gave him our address to my mother's place, and promised him fresh water if he needed it. We made plans to meet up the next day at 10:00 a.m. to correlate on an exit strategy for the next day or possibly after the weekend if that became necessary. He had phone numbers that worked; he had spoken to our boss from the Megastore, and she said she would find a way to come get us if it was possible to get into the city. Katya and I said we wanted in on that plan and then went back to my mother's to get ready for our pool party at my friend's place.

We got dressed quickly and were out the door in a flash. The dusk was impending as we crossed Bourbon Street when, suddenly, we smelled smoke. Looking down toward the Canal Street end of Bourbon we saw great black plumes of ash and cinder, billowing out of an undesignated building. I saw a regular customer from the Megastore heading in that direction; she said that she wanted to see if it looked as if it might spread. Katya and I preferred to be off the street by nightfall, and since we were heading in the opposite direction of the fire, we assumed that we were making the right decision. Upon arrival at our destination, we found the gate cocked open, allowing us unfettered access to the patio area. My friend was in rare form, he was spilling as many drinks as he was quaffing, and cooking the biggest piece of beef I've ever seen. There were other people there, other survivors and friends, all guests of our host's hospitality. I went upstairs to grab a beer, inadvertently meeting my friend's wife. She was not happy, but still, she was very kind, even asking me if some of the food that was being prepared was fit to serve. I said I wasn't a good judge in those matters, instead calling for Katya to help. My friend appeared instead and an argument ensued. I assumed that it was typical marriage quibbles, so I quickly excused myself to the lighter moods down below.

As I took my seat near the pool, I met an extremely drunken unnamed man, as well as another guy named Jack. Soon after that, a young woman and her lovely mother arrived. They seemed happy to be around other kind souls. The food came out of the grill and the feast commenced -- foccacia bread, with rosemary and garlic. Huge slabs of filet cut with the aid of one of the knives I was previously using for defense. There was cold beer, wine, soda, and even salad to start with. We sated ourselves with good conversation, joking; even a cool breeze wafted in from somewhere. We moved over to the pool when night had truly fallen, lit some citronella candles, and tried like hell to just have a good time. We hopped in the pool and the chlorinated water made it all okay, if only for the moment.

Everything was great, some people were a little too drunk by then, but they were still amicable enough. Our host was tanked, but was amazingly able to converse at length about Oscar Wilde and other rare literary pursuits. The young woman, who was far too naïve about the situation she was in, had begun to show traits of cattiness as she got soused. The unnamed drunk man had disappeared; we thought he had gone and passed out somewhere. Jack was constantly coming and going; he lived down the block and was the smartest of us all, as it turned out. He had a veritable bomb shelter just down the street. He had guns, food, water, medicine, and generators -- you name it, he had it. The mother of the young woman went back to her home next door after a while, as she was tired and needed to rest. There was a working phone there, so we all took turns trying to reach anyone we could. All we received was more spotty reception, more near hits and total misses. The real problem began when I found out that I couldn't check my messages, and couldn't leave any either to let people know of our status. Now we really were shipwrecked, locked down for the night in a city becoming more dangerous and abandoned by the hour.

Nevertheless, it seemed that the swimming had eased everyone's nerves. Cool water devoid of disease can do that for a person. We swam and drank, telling each other stories of the strange and wonderful things we had seen and done in the past few days. It was all going well until the liquor took hold -- turning my buddy into a lecherous fiend who didn't care that his wife was just above us, wishing to be away from the crazed wasteland New Orleans had become. He seemed enamored with the drunken young woman, who rebuffed him only enough to make him want more. Eventually, the situation calmed down a bit, and everyone settled into plastic pool furniture, dripping-dry and discussing varied topics. I excused myself to go take a piss in the bushes on the other side of the pool, and returned to find Katya obviously perturbed. The milk had gone sour again, it seemed. Another safe place instantly reduced to shit, and smeared on our shoes.

My blacked-out friend had made a pass at Katya, she told me quietly, while the others carried on and made more drinks. We both agreed that I couldn't create more drama and unneeded attention with a display of machismo at such a crucial time. We began to quietly gather our things, put on our clothes; using hand signals and pointed looks. We were just about to make good on our escape when the young woman, blitzed beyond all recognition, turned into a complete and total waste of skin. It all started when a flashlight beam from across the street was trained on us for an extended period of time. After awhile, it became annoying, but not enough for Katya or me to question it. People were doing that kind of thing to feel safe. We thought: why rock the boat, safe behind an iron fence? Not so for Stupid Bitch, as she will be known from here on out. She decided to ask, with much arrogance:

"Who the **fuck** is doing that?"

She did this in the most obnoxious manner possible, and all hell erupted as a result. Suddenly there was screaming all around. The caretakers of the apartment building my friend lived in were two drunken redneck morons, and they were telling us to shut the fuck up. They started screaming at us to cease the racket we were making or there would be hell to pay. Stupid Bitch replied at the same time as the Unknown Drunkard, suddenly returned from wherever he had disappeared to, and now absolutely too intoxicated to properly speak. She said she was a warrior, and he said he knew kung fu. Neither of them knew anything about either of those subjects, as they were both mentally deficient, and full of liqour on top of that. The rednecks responded with bellowed threats of calling 911, which only made it all the worse.

Cue screams of:

"THERE'S NO 911 YOU STUPID REDNECK BITCH! NOW GET BACK IN YOUR HOUSE BEFORE I MAKE YOU!"

Suddenly, the flashlight across the street had a voice; it was threatening to come down and shoot all of us. Stupid Bitch was not scared; she was a warrior . . . stupid bitch. The Unknown Drunkard decided to lay in some unintelligible nonsense as well, in a sarcastic, superior attitude drawl. Then the rednecks that were within our fortifications produced actual guns, telling us to get the hell out or suffer the consequences. They were overreacting; as it was a state of emergency, and there were no other neighbors home to offend save for them. They could have come and joined us, despite their hee-haw mentality. The fight continued until we were startled by the sound of our host's wife, barricading herself *into* their home. She was literally nailing herself inside, so as to not suffer the same fate we were threatened with.

Katya and I knew that it was time to go. But, we wondered, how? If we had left right in the middle of the turmoil, it would have started an entirely different set of trouble, possibly with BOTH warring factions. We decided to wait, see it out, and hope to everything sacred that we would not be shot. Then my friend started screaming for everyone to chill out, be cool; just one more beer and then the party would be over. There were still more shouts from the rednecks and Stupid Bitch alike, but this passed eventually and silence took hold yet again. Katya and I pretended that we were going to sleep in a lower unoccupied apartment, stealing away down an alley toward the main gate. We hid in the shadows as Stupid Bitch went back to her place next door, sat on her porch, and sobbed vociferously. She started screaming into the night, her mind was obviously blown by the devastation around her, and within her. She screamed some more about how she was a warrior, and how they would all die; how her mother just needed to shut the fuck up and go back to sleep. Then, in the midst of her screed, that Stupid Bitch uttered the most resounding quote of the entire night:

"THEY CAN JUST FUCK MY SUCKING DICK!!!!!"

Hilarious. For so many reasons, it was just hilarious. We waited until she passed out after she had crawled somewhere inside her abode, then went to see if the gate was passable. No luck. I crept back to the pool area, and found that my friend had already passed out on some pool furniture. Luckily, his gate keys were nearby. I grabbed them, unlocked the gate, and Katya held it open. I went back and replaced the keys. As we tried to leave -- blinding light -- the rednecks were upon us, asking questions, with guns drawn. We told them how we needed to escape from that asylum, and how those people in there were crazy and drunk and stupid. The rednecks agreed with us, of course, and let us go on our way. We hurried down the street to Esplanade Avenue, and then over to Decatur Street for what would turn out to be the longest walk of our lives.

The nights before were romantic and curious; now it was harrowing and surreal. There weren't even candles to light a path; no flashlights to illuminate our trek. It was just a bombed-out city, our little $1.99 flashlight, two knives, and Katya and me, walking slowly in total darkness. Blocks seemed like city lengths, sounds reverberated from nowhere; startling us, making us stop -- frozen. We feared that waiting predators were at every corner, and every enclave. We knew exactly what a zombie movie was like at this point. If it moved, it was an enemy until otherwise quantified. Back to back, we inched toward St. Ann Street, hoping that those things we heard creeping around out there were just abandoned pets scavenging food. Then we saw sirens in the distance. The cops were out, and just as dangerous as any gang member or looter. We knew that a curfew was in effect, and so we snaked through the Quarter, going street-to-street, and then corner-to-corner. Every light, every sound was a threat, and so when we finally saw the flicker of my mother's gas powered Bevolo flame in the distance, we breathed heavy sighs of relief.

So it was more of the same -- more radio, more sweat, and more shock and worry. Our Mayor, Ray Nagin, screaming in desperation on the radio, and into the night. We listened to families leaving on-air messages to their loved ones; whether missing, dead, or evacuated. The radio announcers were as lost as anyone else, and yet they still maintained service to the public despite the stories of tragedy and hopelessness they heard in their twelve hour shifts. We sat and listened silently, as we had for the last few days, soaking in the pathos inherent in the whole affair. We hoped that Bob was safe, that he would come see us tomorrow, and that we could all find a way out of the situation unscathed and in good health. We hoped that no one tried to invade our fort during the night; that we wouldn't have to hurt someone or even worse, get hurt. Hope was all we had at that point, options appearing and disappearing as quickly as the helicopters that were constantly scanning the area for anything and everything, whether alive or dead.

We barely slept that night, even less than nights before. Visions of terrors danced in our heads when Morpheus embraced us, if even for a moment.

Chapter Six

Thursday, September 1, 2005

– This Day Means Escape –

After a night of fettered tossing and basting in our own juices, we finally peeled ourselves from slumber. The previous night's adventure in zombie-land was still playing back -- sepia-tone denial and attendant shock in tow. We turned on the radio, drank warm bottled water, and stared at the floor for long moments. Nothing better to do. We made motions of getting dressed, tried to eat....

No way, the food would not have any of that nonsense. We knew that our meeting with Bob was fast approaching, yet we were still slow and rattled to motivate. The first stirrings of our own damage, emotional damage, were becoming hard to navigate past, small occurrences causing bigger fights than were necessary. We quibbled and argued, all while attempting to keep our wits sharp should the craziness outside decide to inquire within. Since I basically changed clothes without bathing, save for a good flossing and brushing, I decided to step outside and see what changes the night had wrought this time.

The first thing I noticed was that everyone I saw, everything in motion, was going in one direction -- towards Canal St. This was the real moment of escape, as anyone and everyone seemed to be making their final bid to either stay put or get the hell outta there. At the time I figured that it was the heat, maybe the threat of violence that was making such a final exodus occur. No, as one woman told me, it was the threat of disease. Terrible and potent, borne from the stagnating waters surrounding our island, the airwaves were alive with horror stories and warnings new and fresh. As I went back inside, the radio was already confirming her story and my darkest fear:

It seemed that all of the old favorites, Scarlet Fever, Malaria, Dysentery, and Hepatitis were making a comeback. A hundred years, some had not been here in a hundred years, they told us, and now it was time to get scared. There were no defenses against this threat, not this time. Well, unless you looted all the right medicines in a moment of prescience at the pharmacy, but we hadn't. They gave us the fear and we set it alight, great flashing coronas of doubt and animal fear taking hold for the first real time. Whether it was true was not really the matter in question at the time. Pure survival mode took over and as we asked ourselves the one question we had failed to address, there was a knock at the door.

It was Bob, looking tired and disheveled, but rather chipper considering the circumstances. He came inside, and we told him about the new crease in the situation. He laid some rather heavy news at our feet as well, something that killed our previous plans stone cold. We were going to have our boss from the Megastore drive over the Crescent City Connection to hopefully pick us up and get us out. Bob had been told since our last meeting that NO ONE was being allowed in on the bridges unless they were approved search and rescue workers. This changed the situation dramatically in only a few scant minutes, but I knew that something had to be done. Somebody had to have information about where she could come rescue us. We knew that salvation had to be available without having to resort to descending into the abyss that the Superdome had become -- much less the Convention Center. We sat and thought about what options were open to us, what were the logical moves from there? I came up with the idea of going closer to the mouth of the beast, to see what the media and lawmen knew on Canal St. Yeah, Canal St., that's right . . . it was the only idea I had.

We drank more water, got our nerve up for the trek, armed and ready as usual. We moved out, heading towards the Megastore for another pass to see if anyone had breached the perimeter. No dice for the looters. We were again amazed at the Megastore standing strong, while the rest of the city seemed to be weeping. We walked down Decatur St. to the split at N. Peters St. and took N. Peters towards the Canal Place Mall. You could see that the mall had not fared well in the storm. The upper levels of the building were shorn completely off, the lower levels smashed and looted. All of the display windows for the corner location of Saks Fifth Avenue were a riot of mannequin parts, shining cubes of safety glass and the few remaining scraps of clothing that must not have been in fashion for the looter on the go in this modern world.

We stopped to speak to a group of tourists recently evicted from their hotel suites long enough to realize that this truly was the kingdom of the blind. It seemed that the hotel they were lodging in had told them that they were now a liability and that buses were being dispatched for them. All the tourists had to do, the hotel manager told them, was to go and wait on the curb outside. We knew that there were no such buses coming anytime in the near future, but we just didn't have the heart to tell them. They had already been waiting for over four hours; some of them seemed not to realize that this was not a normal shuttle as they were complaining about the holdup. We couldn't help, so we bade them farewell, and good luck. We knew that they would most likely wind up having to wade down to the Superdome, somewhere we were hoping we didn't have to find ourselves.

As we came to the corner of Canal and N. Peters St., I was first struck by the amount of people assembled there. There were media vans everywhere, mostly in the center of the street. It was a mad scene, people running everywhere, other locals like us making their way across Canal into the areas that we were determined not to tread. Suddenly, a young man appeared next to me, asking me if I know where "that" restaurant is that is open and serving food. I had to honestly choke back a laugh at this point; he seemed to not have a clue as to what was going on. I told him as much, that the only two places open were bars, that they only had beers and cigarettes if he was lucky. He smelled like he hadn't bathed since way before the storm or possibly that he had waded through the disgusting floodwaters. I stepped back, trying to get away from his funky odor and suspicious demeanor. He asked again about any open businesses, not seeming to grasp even the simple news I had just told him. I told him he was out of luck, joking that if he found fresh hot food to come tell *us* where it was. As I was telling him goodbye and trying to get rid of him, I heard Katya say something close to:

"What the FUCK!?!?!"

Next thing I know, there is a Police cruiser at my knees, literally. There is a Cop brandishing a 12 gauge shotgun directly at my face, screaming that we need to hit the ground:

"NOW MOTHERFUCKER!!!!! NOW!!!!!"

Needless to say, we all hit the ground. Katya, Bob, myself, and even our stinky friend. I was so ready to just lose it at this point, words fail me. I really thought that we were going to the only place worse than the Superdome or the Convention Center. I thought we were going to jail, or possibly somewhere worse.

Suddenly, as quick as we were down, we were up again. He, the cop, he's telling us to flee. He's telling Katya, Bob and I to get the FUCK out of there. We do just that. As we hit the center of Canal St., we turn and see that it was our inquisitively smelly friend they were after. They were beating him senseless, the cop from before and the two other cars full of cops that had come screeching in. Roughly 6 or so officers delivered a serious beating onto this man. They were stomping and screaming and threatening and humiliating him so seriously that I remember thinking that he must have done something horribly wrong. I didn't realize until much later that you didn't have to do much to get beaten that way, considering the circumstances.

We decided to walk down the center of the street, through the media circus in hopes of avoiding any further nasty surprises. As we got to the cars and reporters setting up their remote feeds and unfiltered satellite relays, we had to divert onto Canal St. proper as there was simply too much to navigate. We scanned the throng for a CNN news van, maybe the reporter who interviewed us Monday was there, and maybe he knew something valuable. No such luck, as the CNN van was locked and empty. We walked a bit further, all the while marveling at the fury that Katrina had unleashed upon Canal St. Some hotels were unscathed save for some minor window and awning damage. Some had their entire facades torn off. We saw bemused tourists, drinking bottled water in dirty boxer shorts looking from five flights up at us down below. We saw the countless shops that were obviously looted clean, the debris in the streets appearing far too man made to be Katrina even in her worst hour. We saw the water in the streets, getting dirtier and higher the further you went towards Claiborne Ave. We knew that this meant the stories were true. The rest of the city was submerged in one way or another; we really were on an island. You could tell that Canal St. was being used as a makeshift dividing line, as there was barely anyone going into the French Quarter, only people coming out.

As we were standing in the middle of the street, debating our next move, a stout guy in shorts and a t-shirt comes up and queries if he can ask us a few questions. He says his name is Klaus and he works for the German News Agency. His head is shaved and he looks really out of place, so much so that we figure he must be telling the truth. We tell him sure; we'll answer all the questions he wants. We tell him we have some of our own. He walks down the block a bit to jump over the rank flood water in the gutters, where it is at its slimmest point. He approaches us as any good journalist should, notepad at the ready, pen in hand. He asks the usual litany of questions that everyone asked each other since the storm:

Why did we stay?

Were we from a flooded area?

Did we lose everything?

Had we seen evidence of looting and violence?

If we had, were we direct victims of such action?

Why were we staying, considering the way the situation had turned out by this point?

As he asked that last question, all three of us responded in unison with different explanations as to why we were standing in front of him at that very moment. We were trying to leave, the cop had a gun and that guy he was beating smelled really bad and there was looting everywhere and desperate acts of violence and people were losing their minds and decency and we just wanted a hot shower and some real food and it was too damn hot and the threat of disease and the fuckin' zombies man, the fuckin' zombies....

He took all of this in for a moment, realizing that we were telling him that he caught us at a pretty pivotal moment for the three of us. He responded by offering to drive us out of town, in one hour, to Baton Rouge where he was headed anyway. All he asked in return for his services was "the story". We assured him that there was no problem -- we would give him all of the story he could handle. He told us to go and gather what we would need to evacuate with, and to meet him back at that spot in one hour. We could not believe what was happening, but we still moved as if we were being chased back towards my mother's place to gather the cats and the few items we had that mattered there. As we hustled back that way, we figured out the amount of time it would take to grab our things and make our way back to Canal St. and Klaus in the hour provided. As we reached my mother's, Bob set off for his place which was just around the corner.

We ran inside and attacked our belongings, gathering everything we needed into two packs in less than ten minutes. Wrangling the cats into their carrier was a little harder, but after a few minutes we were able to coax them in and we were ready to make good our escape. Katya went out to the patio to see if there was any type of cart that would help us move faster and move more bags easily, returning with a broken Igloo cooler.

The wheels and the handle worked just fine though, so we were able to pile our bags and the cat carrier on top, giving the cats a perfect parade-like view through the French Quarter.

As I stepped outside to look for Bob, I could see that the descent was still in full effect. Everyone I saw at that point looked haggard, beaten, and desperate. It was palpable, the sense that anything and everything was up for grabs; there really were no rules at that moment. We were back to the law of the jungle. It was the primordial state of KAOS I had always searched for, only realizing too late that I was unprepared for it in this place, in this time. Escape was the only option now, there was more than just my well-being at stake here and I knew the responsibility that entailed. I knew that our window of opportunity was closing so I scanned the street again for Bob and there he was. Here was our moment of truth. All we had to do was one final jaunt through the Quarter, one last sad waltz with our fair city. So off we went.

We made it all the way down Dauphine St. to Iberville St., when we came upon a group of cops who told us to cross over somewhere else. We obliged. With visions of our earlier encounter still making us cringe, we opted to get the hell away from anyone holding a weapon if we could help it. We went down to Bourbon St. -- no go. Too much water in the street, plus the smell was that of death, of rotten meat and shellfish, garbage and diseased nightmares. We went down to Royal St. -- same story there; the pharmacy on the corner was compromised and looted clean. You could see that someone had decided to destroy what was left in the store, knocking the display shelves over like dominoes in some pointless display of random destruction. We made our way to Chartres St., finding an alley that was relatively clear of water. It was clear enough for me to ferry the cats through, and I could tell that they were as scared as we were. The smell was so bad at this point that we had to put rags over our faces to avoid gagging. Bob started saying that if Klaus had left us, he was going to just sit down and cry. I knew how he felt. After three days of the aftermath of Katrina, I was at that point as well. I just held out that this was going to be the one thing that stayed true in all of this. It was.

We hit Canal St., and there's Klaus' car. No Klaus, but his car is still there, so I hung out while Katya went to search for our erstwhile savior. Bob sidled up, obviously ready to just wait it out with me at the car. We looked around and noticed that the media is in full swing. Cameras and lights and action everywhere, some reporters maintaining those camera-friendly smiles despite the horror and desperation surrounding them. Suddenly, Katya reappeared, saying that Klaus was on the way. As we saw him come around a car, we breathed sighs of relief. He walked up, smiled, and said that the action was go. A rev of the engine and then the rain began.

Yes, you heard that right. Almost on cue it started raining, another bizarre twist in a long string of strangeness. As we silently made our way out of the French Quarter into the C.B.D. we noticed the damage Katrina had visited on that part of the city. More broken high-rise windows, more looted stores, more evacuees moving away from the city they called home. We hit the Crescent City Connection getting a first real look at the Superdome, its once recognizable white dome a peeled mess of adhesives and broken tiles. We saw the first groups of National Guard rolling in, high-powered rifles and night vision scopes at the ready for their first night in the wasteland. Then we came to a roadblock on the bridge, cops and military guard ready to deter the people crazy or desperate enough to cross the bridge on foot or bicycle. Most of the people we saw were camped out under the highways, but some were actually trying to make it out by any means necessary. As we sailed through the roadblock, the rain intensified, but only long enough to make our last glimpse of New Orleans, the city we both grew up in, our home... bittersweet.

At this point we all kind of clammed up. Shock set in hard for our entire ride through the West Bank, Jefferson Parish, and then onto the highway towards Baton Rouge. There were some tears, but only enough to be expected. We had survived. We had escaped the belly of the beast. Now we were going to tell our story, and make our next move. Little did we know . . . the adventure was far from over.

"Birds in futile quest for flight moving backwards in slow motion."

"More trees everywhere; water, water, and more water."

"The echo of rescue helicopters puréed their way into the psyches of the survivors."

"Everyone I saw at that point looked haggard, beaten, and desperate."

"One final jaunt through the Quarter; one last sad waltz with our fair city."

"Blasted mortar, broken dreams and hope and cares."

"Discarded fishing boats littered the highways; what became of their captains?"

"Add every detail I have chronicled up until now and then smash it to tinder."

Chapter Seven

September 1 - 4, 2005

– Let's Get the Hell Outta Here! –

While Klaus steered us out of the twitching rape that New Orleans had become, we marveled at the far-reaching power of Katrina, how she had turned the entire city and the surrounding parishes into swamps, junkyards, killing fields, and refugee camps. Thunderdome. We watched as the National Guard rolled into town on the highway opposite from us for the first real time since the storm had hit -- trucks and troops and guns and solemn looks. We made the obligatory proclamations of how good it was to be out, how much we looked forward to hot showers, regular food, soft beds and air conditioning. We slipped into moments of silence, worrying, wondering, and pondering.

As the last bands of Katrina related disruption to the scenery disappeared behind us, our attitudes began to shift down a bit. We started to give Klaus a bit of background on ourselves and got to know him a bit better. He was a German journalist, working here in the States, covering mostly political concerns in Washington, D. C. He said he found it numbing, as there was no real density there, no weight to what he was assigned to cover. He'd been on reports abroad that had moved him; made him feel that there was more to be seen and done in the most tangible of ways. He had sort of, um, disobeyed his assignment, telling his editors that he was going to Mississippi; instead he went to New Orleans.

He somehow knew that there was a very important part of the story playing out there, one that at that moment demanded attention and mercy. Then he met us and there was a chance to actually do something, so he did. He met others as well while he waited for us, getting quotes, gathering phone numbers to call for them, and offering assistance if possible. He called their families, their coworkers, bosses, boyfriends, girlfriends, and acquaintances. He told them that they were okay when he saw them, although their vacation was ruined, but that they were alive. He told them that they were trying to get out, that their honeymoon was memorable, and no way were they naming any kid of theirs Katrina. He told them that they might not be back to work as scheduled from the convention, although they had some insane pictures to share when they did get home. He made call after call after call, always getting someone on the phone, and always making someone very happy. It seemed our savior was just exactly that, both physically and mentally. To be around that type of behavior turned us all around -- we started to make small talk, and even joked around a bit.

As we hit the city limits of Baton Rouge proper, Klaus told us that we were going to get some food, and then head on over to L. S. U. campus to the Journalism building. Once in the city, it was amazing to see the amount of traffic and congestion that Baton Rouge was experiencing. The streets were gagged; emptied gas pumps covered in black plastic sacks. Some stores had lines out into the street, more blank stares and paranoia. Klaus pulled into the first place he saw that didn't have a throng of evacuees crowding it and it turned out that it was McDonald's... urk. After about a nanosecond of deliberation, due to our aversions to fast food, we realized that those soft drink machines had ice in them, and that the food at least smelled good at that moment. We ate our meals thankfully, as Klaus had paid for them, but we still ate quickly nonetheless. As we exited the restaurant we decided to grab a quick smoke despite the fact that the rain had kicked up again. A gentleman also smoking at the ashtray outside was dressed in hospital scrubs and sporting a look that suggested that he had also just escaped from the same dark place that we had been rescued from. We were right. He told us that he was a staff member at one of the hospitals in the city, one of the larger ones. He was also there for four days. We asked him if it was bad there: were the rumors true? He replied that it was horrific, the bodies of the deceased patients piling up in the hallways sometimes at the rate of two to three an hour. The staff was giving themselves injections of complex B vitamins and saline to stave off exhaustion and dehydration, working all the time -- no sleep til salvation. Then there were the gangs of thugs, storming the entrances, they wanted the drugs and had the guns to get them. Police finally arrived, but not before panic and despair had set in. You could tell that he was still in the grip of that fear, his glazed eyes and too-calm demeanor belying his true state of mind.

The rain started to let up a bit, and Klaus said we had to make good time back to L.S.U. so we could do our interview, so it was time to go. We told our shell-shocked acquaintance goodbye and piled back into the car to make good on our promise of "the story". The traffic was tight and angry, but we made it to L.S.U. campus with little trouble, considering the circumstances. As Klaus gained entrance to the Journalism building there, we sat and figured out what we were going to do after the interview was over. We tried the phones, but there was no reception. Now that we were out, well, we had to wait.

So we occupied ourselves by watching the college students go about their daily lives that we thought had nothing to do at all with hurricanes. Then Klaus returned and said we should go over to the campus center to get cold drinks and relax, as the journalism building was too occupied at the moment. We walked over and tried the phones again, grabbed our snacks and drinks, then found a table to sit for our interview.

As we answered questions and gave explanations for some of our answers, Klaus pointed out that some of the kids walking around campus had pained looks on their faces. They were the ones with nametags slapped on, the ones with tired shoulders. It seemed that because of the hurricane the campus football stadium was being used as a makeshift triage area and the students had been given a three day break from classes. The kids we were seeing with the nametags, they were the ones who took those three days to volunteer to help the sick and infirmed who had just been brought out of the disaster area. We marveled at their sacrifice and giving natures, and then answered more questions. After some time, Klaus just listened to us, letting us tell him just about the entire story you have read up until this point. He took copious notes and always asked the right questions; when we finished it felt good. It was almost as if we had caught up to the shock for a moment. Almost. After that, we were able to relax and learn more about Klaus. We came to realize that he was as wary of strangers as we were at first, but once he got to know us, he had no problems ferrying us out of harms way. We told him how much we sincerely appreciated his act of kindness, and he responded cool and calm. I could tell that he wasn't trying to seem as if he was full of himself, or show that he was pained by what he had seen in New Orleans. He handled the situation better than any other person I met from the outside. He told us that he was probably going back the next day to rescue more people, and try to persuade others to do the same. Words fail me when it comes to explaining the amount of respect and gratitude I have for Klaus Marre. He had saved us from any number of indignities and horrors; it rounded out that he was also one hell of a nice guy.

Right around that time Bob started to try the phone lines again, failing to reach our boss. He opted to try the Assistant Manager of the Megastore, Kelly, with glorious results. They were on the way immediately, and the next step was upon us. As we waited, a woman came out of the university center building with a disturbed look on her face. Katya asked her if she was okay, and the woman just flat-out broke down crying.

She was trapped in the Convention Center for three days and couldn't find her husband. She had taken her dog with her there and the roving gangs had threatened to kill her and steal the dog, maybe just raping her in the process for the hell of it. There was the same rumor we had heard of the levees being blown and the city being drowned, only in her situation it was much more horrific. At night, when the gunfire started in the blackness of the Convention Center, the sound was as that of fast, rushing water. This sent those not already hysterical over the gunfire into mass lunacy, and so, people were trampled; the elderly and children were included. She said that the bodies were everywhere, and so was the unnerving threat of joining them... or worse. I excused myself from the table after a moment, not out of selfishness, but to check on Bob, who had been sitting in front of the university center waiting for someone to arrive. He asked me to wait there while he used the facilities and, almost as soon as he left, our boss Kirsten arrived. Kelly had finally gotten through to her and was also waiting further down the road. Kirsten said there was a safe place to go, and so we gladly accepted the offer. After many hugs and handshakes we were all together and it seemed that a plan was already in action. We were going to New Iberia, Louisiana, to a safe place in the country where there was more than enough room and hospitality.

We met up with Kelly and her boyfriend Trevva in a supermarket parking lot, hopping into their truck to complete the next leg in our journey. We rode through Lafayette, then into the sugarcane fields of New Iberia, further away from the chaos. Our arrival at the home of Trevva's family friends, the Grows', was greeted with smiles and warmth. These were simple country folk, doing their Lords work in the most sincere way they could. They told us there was food, showers, clean beds for us to use, and a pool to swim in should we care to take a dip. Katya and I had a room to ourselves and let the cats loose from their incarceration, unpacked a bit, and then went outside to try the phones and make contact with whatever family members we could. As I sat and drank some wonderfully cold beer and dialed number after number on the phone, I watched the rest of our party swim and try to relax as best they could. I finally got my sister on the phone and she had many numbers for me to call, namely my family members in Mandeville: my mother, grandparents, aunt, and brother-in-law. She also had numbers for me to call in the neighboring city of Jeanerette -- I had distant relatives there as well. After calling my mother and breaking down a bit over the details of our respective trials at the hands of Katrina, I made plans to get there as soon as a better idea of just what was going on came about. A swim in the pool and a few more beers later I was ready to go to sleep. Being in a strange house, no matter how safe, was disconcerting at first. When I finally was able to close my eyes and start to doze, I was started back to waking by hallucinations of flashing lights and great whooshing noises. It seemed that the helicopters, while not in the sky, were still there.

The next day was slow to start at first; we lounged in bed until mid-morning, enjoying the fact that we had nothing serious forcing us out of bed. We started out by first taking hot showers and eating fresh food that was plentiful and ours to do with as we saw fit. That done, our attention turned to the television. The first real, serious look at what the rest of the world had been watching was hard to stomach. It was far worse than we had even feared while trapped in the city; the horrifying images replaying over and over and over. We saw Lakeview, Uptown, St. Bernard, and New Orleans east, everywhere -- submerged. The looting and the desperation; screams of despair from the Convention Center and the Superdome. Children lost and crying for anything decent, anything safe and protecting. National Guardsmen corralling the evacuees on highways and curbsides, the mad rush of humanity into buses that were too long in coming. Sandbags airborne, dropping into football field-sized breaches in the levees that Katrina had flooded. We even glimpsed ourselves for a moment, from our interview with CNN on the previous Monday; it was surreal and familiar in equal doses. We watched as the first stirrings of political dissent ramped up in all directions. Nagin, Blanco, Brown, Bush and the rest were all making their initial bids to be The One With No Guilt.

After watching our worst fears visually confirmed on television for far too long, we decided to busy ourselves with the first of a long and painful list of concerns. We gained limited access to the internet, sending out basic communications to friends and family. We then earned our keep by helping with some basic household chores for Mrs. Grow; we didn't want to appear ungrateful for her hospitality. We called as many friends and family members as we could, but at that point the lines were stuttered at best. After that, it was more CNN, more waiting, more despair, and more anger. During that time, Kelly told me that they were going to Human Services in town late that night to apply for aid, mostly the emergency food stamp program that had been launched in Katrina's wake. I agreed that I should go with them and later that night, I overheard Trevva and Mr.

Grow talking about a car that was up for sale. It sounded like a good deal, one that would help to get Katya and I further with our eventual departure. We knew that the coming month or so out of town would be almost impossible to endure without transportation and this looked like a costly but assured way to remedy such concerns. I inquired about the car and the price was right. Plans were made for purchase later that week when funds were easier to procure.

Not too long after that we made a run to Wal-Mart and then the Food Stamp office. Sitting in that office was as edifying as it was crushing to the soul. There were families, some sleeping in the plastic chairs, all gathering like tribes to tell their particular stories about their moments in Hell. Even though the visit there was thankfully brief, it still drove the magnitude and scope of Katrina home in a uniquely personal fashion. Arriving back at the Grows' house, I cracked open the first of many beers of the night, realizing that strong drink was in high order for me to sleep. Everyone except for Trevva and I headed for bed, so He and I hung out for a bit, talking and drinking. After he realized that it was nigh on sunrise, Trevva excused himself to bed, leaving me to finish my beer alone and head to sleep myself. I decided to catch a bit more CNN, to see what the latest developments were in our deserted hometown.

I don't know if it was the drink, the effects of shock or just simple exhaustion, but that was the first moment that I faltered. There was a report on CNN about Charity Hospital, how the doctors there were almost broken, the dead bodies of patients were everywhere; it was obvious that things were getting extremely ugly there. As I watched the footage of rescue helicopters hauling people off of the adjacent roof of Tulane Hospital, while leaving the patients on gurneys from Charity sitting there, waiting for hours, I lost it. Simple as that. I quickly shut down the television and threw my empties away, tears welling in my eyes. As soon as I hit the room we were using to sleep in, the floodgates opened and I let them. It all came crashing down, the fact that while we were safe we were as lost as anyone else in all of this. The force of the revelation hit me with such ferocity that I couldn't deny it, fight it, or do anything but simply weep at all that had been lost, and all that was yet to endure for everyone involved. I drifted to sleep as the sun rose, knowing full well that the real nightmares would be waiting for me when I finally got out of bed whether I liked it or not.

After getting up far too late the next day, some good news was at hand. Two more survivors from the Megastore had made contact, having escaped from the city two full days later than we did. It turned out that they had also befriended some journalists who helped them to escape just as we had two days previous. Brian and Angela were their names and they were on their way to New Iberia. Of course, we watched more CNN, made more phone calls, and planned a bit further into the future as to what Katya and I were going to do in the coming weeks. I finally reached my Uncle Stan, who was in Jeanerette with a host of other distant relatives who had also escaped Katrina. We started to make plans to stay there for a night until my brother-in-law was able to drive up and bring us back to Mandeville. This was cut short by the arrival of Brian and Angela and the celebration that followed, albeit a subdued one. They were obviously shaken by their experience, so we left them to shower and grab something to eat before pestering them with our concerns and questions. The important thing was that they were okay, which seemed to be true, if only in the physical sense. As the time grew near for us to pack, I noticed that there was some sort of disruption brewing between Kelly and Mrs. Grow outside; there were hurt looks and a few tears flowing from Kelly. I went outside to let them know that my uncle was on the way and that we could take someone with us to help keep the flow of evacuees from becoming too intrusive. At that point I thought that we would take Bob with us, keep the little group we had formed intact, but I was made aware of a wrinkle that changed the plan.

As I said before, these were country folk. Mrs. Grow respectfully informed us that since Angela was of African descent, she might not feel too welcome in their home once the neighbors and, most importantly, Mr. Grow saw that she was as such. I reserved judgment at that moment since it was more important to me to not have to go through any more drama that soon. It was their home after all, and if that was how it was, all I could do was try to make sure we made it out of there without fanfare or bad vibes. This made the situation hard all over again, as Mrs. Grow didn't want to hurt her feelings, didn't want to make her feel uncomfortable after she had just been through such trying times. So I did the only thing that was right; I told them that she was welcome at any place I was going -- end of problem. My family is not of that mindset, so that was that. I went inside, Katya and I gathered our bags and cats and quietly appraised Angela of the situation. She was ready in moments, so we waited for my uncle to arrive. He rolled into the driveway at just the right moment, so we said our goodbyes and promised to return soon to purchase the car that was for sale, and then we were off. Not too long afterward we were at my Aunt Sue's house eating home cooked food and swapping stories of insanity and loss with my other family members who were also sheltered there. As the night descended, we realized that where there was communication just a town over, here there was none. We were afforded one house phone that barely worked, no internet, no place to sleep except for the floor, and no place to let the cats out of their carrier. Luckily, I reached my sister in Texas without trouble and she had some decent news. My brother-in-law Jason was heading through Jeanerette late that very night and he would happily pick us up so that at least we could free the cats and sleep in beds again, not to mention see my mother. Mandeville had been hit hard, but this was still preferable to being stopped in our tracks completely, as we were.

During our wait, the toll was visibly registering on Angela; she was crying a bit and seemed to have no appetite. She was in the same situation Katya was in -- she had no idea as to the welfare or whereabouts of her family and it was weighing them both down. I assured her that once we had a stable situation, relatively speaking, she would be afforded all means available to find her family that we had ourselves. She relaxed after that and she and Katya stretched out on the carpeted floor of my Aunt's dining room. Jason arrived in the middle of the night, unshaven and erratic, but visibly happy to see us. It was good to have visited with some of my family, but it was time to go see my mother and try to move forward yet a bit more. We made the trek in good time, arriving in Mandeville under cover of darkness; Katrina had broadsided the area as we would come to find out the next day under scrutiny of the sun. There was but one light working at their house with a generator loud enough to wake the dead powering it and very little else. As we pulled up to the house, I could see the trees that were scattered everywhere, some resting square in the center of people's homes. Luckily for my family, their house was scraped up a bit, but still structurally solid. I briefly hugged my mother who had risen at the sound of our arrival. She was groggy, but happy to see us alive and in one piece. This was where the pieces of the puzzle would be assembled, I thought, and aside from the lack of electricity and water, things were good... or so they seemed at the time.

What we were to learn was that damage comes in all forms, all shapes, and all sizes. There were still many that we had not yet been party to, but that would come in due time. We were not out of the woods yet; in fact, we were only just beginning our adventure.

We fell asleep to the thrum of box fans powered by the diesel beast rattling incessantly in the yard, and it was still preferable to those damn helicopters.

Chapter Eight

September 5 - 14, 2005

– Time Keeps On Slippin',
Slippin', Slippin'... –

With just enough sleep to make rising tolerable, my sister's home came alive slowly on the day following our arrival. My mother, brother-in-law Jason, Katya, Angela and I all made use of what small amenities there were, what with the water and electricity being down and out at the time. There was food, cold drinks (beer included) in ice chests and enough work to keep us occupied for the next few days until my sister arrived. In just the week or so since the storm, Mandeville had actually struggled into action; righting leaning power lines, starting removal of trees and garbage, and reopening stores so people could buy basic supplies.

As we sat around and caught up with each other as to the events of the past weeks respective adventures, I started to realize that everyone had suffered in some fashion or another. While Katya, Angela and I had survived the chaos that the French Quarter and surrounding areas had become, my family had weathered the storm in another, yet equally horrifying way. As we sat on the patio in the scalding damp of a typically smothering September afternoon, Jason relived his experience of sitting on the same patio the night of the storm. He recounted, with disturbing lucidity, how he listened as the sound of snapping lumber came ever closer, signaling the approach and ferocity of the storm. He was in awe, he said, as he could hear the trees, the wide expanses of trees dying . . . he knew that all it would take was one errant trunk landing in the wrong place, spelling doom for the entire house and the occupants. He was right. All you had to do to confirm his suspicions was walk around his house, much less walk out into the street. There were trees, broken, stripped of bark, and twisted into corkscrew formations EVERYWHERE. Most were in neighboring yards, crashed over their fences; some were sticking squarely out of houses, sometimes more than one or even two. The roads were impassable in some places, not that there was anywhere to go anyway. The city was, for all intents and purposes, on lockdown, especially after nightfall. Luckily, the section of Mandeville they had moved into was beyond the reach of the major flooding but that would be the only good fortune to smile upon them. The entire region was sharing the same fate as every other nearby: waking up from a knockout blow, and barely able to remember its name or how it got there.

After letting the obvious sink in, we started to relate our personal tales. The encounters, misadventures, hopes and fears that Katrina had run each of us through.

Jason told us why my grandparents weren't there anymore, and why they had gone to Texas to find refuge with a cousin. It turned out that they had lost their home in Lakeview, the one they had lived in since right after the end of World War Two. After enduring the storm and the unimaginable stress it had caused on their aged minds and bodies, to learn of the loss of everything they had ever accumulated was just too much. Petty squabbling and lack of routine had caused a rift between the entire household, including my mother and my aunt. After much hand-wringing and hourly phone calls to my sister, who was still in Texas herself, it was agreed they would be far more comfortable in a place amenable to their delicate situation, and luckily we had cousins in Houston. Jason had scooped us up on his return from dropping my grandparents and aunt off, which explained why he appeared so harried at the time. Also there at the house for a short time was a woman named Marie, who had a miniature dog, too many prescriptions\ medications and more neuroses then I care to recount. She was a refugee from down the street; we secretly hoped she was going back that way sooner than later due to her incessant babbling and bad timing. Luckily for us and for her, she went back home a few days later and we resumed what passed for normal family concerns.

We spent the next few days cleaning the house, clearing the yard, and moving the boxes and furniture that were still where I had left them when I had helped them move in a couple of days before the storm. During this time, the power came back on to hearty cheers and the cranking up of the air conditioning. Throughout this, we continued to attempt communications, both to our friends and family who we still hadn't gotten through to. Good news came when it was discovered that Katya's family had all made it out safe and well enough for their trouble. They had persevered through a week of the aftermath in their home in the Broadmoor area of town, despite the three feet of disgusting flood water that surrounded them, not to mention the numerous fires razing the area. They had made it to Baton Rouge, to a place called False River. Plans were made to rendezvous with them after we bought the car from the Grows that we had planned on. You could see Katya relax measurably after that, it was if the weight of Atlas lifted from her shoulders and it definitely helped attitudes to soften.

Another couple of days passed and my sister arrived home with my two nephews, Tyler and Paul. Just seeing them made things come into focus for me, their innocence and love for me erasing almost all traces of shock and horror. As we had our first "family" dinner that night, everyone seemed jovial and relaxed, even becoming loose enough to talk about the current state of affairs without drama or fanfare. We had drinks and smokes afterward, retelling some stories, remembering others that had been forgotten or otherwise buried. At this point, about a week and a half had passed since the storm and Angela was still worried about her family -- they still weren't all accounted for. Cell phones still didn't work that well and there was no land line phone. Same went for internet access, so it was hit and miss for all of us. Angela was holding up quite well, even helping with the care of my nephews during the day when everyone else in the house was preoccupied with other responsibilities. She came through in a very crucial way for my family, and although I guess we were even considering that we were putting her up, I could never convey how much I appreciate her helping as she did. She is one of the most kind-hearted women I've met, never letting on as to how hard all of it was on her. I'll always remember listening to music with Angela on the patio, drunk out of my gourd, as the blackness of Mandeville surrounded us and our conversations.

Then the day finally came when almost enough money for the car materialized. Almost, in that we had pooled every last cent we had between us and yet it was still not enough to pay the various fees and taxes, plus the cost of the car itself. After speaking with a few different people about FEMA and the other forms of relief becoming available, we decided that any help from those parties would be too long in coming for us to count them as funds for the car. Right when it seemed that we were going to be marooned in Mandeville for the entirety of our evacuation, a light shined on us from California in the form of one of Katya's aunts. We were offered enough money to buy the car and at least make a go of getting out of the wreckage the entire state of Louisiana had become. A couple more phone calls later and we were on our way back to New Iberia to pay off Mr. Grow and drive away clean and free, on our own. We arrived in New Iberia early enough to haggle with Western Union about their closed locations, cash my paychecks and count our pennies in order to complete the sale. After an hour or so of racing around, we had the car, and the license plate. Now we had the way out we had needed so desperately during our time in the Quarter. We headed back to Mandeville with dusk at our backs and hope in our hearts for the first real time since our escape. No matter what, we were now the true masters of our destinies; we were in charge of where we went and how we got there. It wasn't until we missed an exit and found ourselves having to go hours out of our way that we discovered yet another maddening wrinkle in our tapestry of inconvenience... the car overheated every so often at will, we were stuck somewhere on the Baton Rouge highway, and Katya's cell phone was getting sporadic calls through at best. Another hour or two of oil changes, epithets, and psychotic breakdowns. Then, after much gnashing of teeth, we were back on our way.

Another facet of the entire experience was the constant state of looking, feeling and actually being, lost. Sometimes all at once. The more we traveled during our evacuation, the more we would figure that out along with all of the other new and unwelcome discoveries about life in the wake of Katrina.

After returning to our base in Mandeville, Katya and I started to hash out what the plan would be now that we had a car at our disposal. We had to see her family; of that much we were certain, but where to after that? We had many opportunities offered to us; it was making them all fit that became a problem. We could have gone to Austin, Colorado, Memphis, California, Kansas City, even as far as London, England. As the days became almost another week, the wait started to take its toll on everyone in the house. My mother was not doing well in all of this, what with her worries about her parents and sister, her distance from her apartment in the French Quarter, and the rest of her fears we all shared at the time about the fate of the city in general.

You have to appreciate the gravity of the situation we were in at that point. The local newspaper, small as it was, was being delivered although the news it contained was sad and frightening. Radio held little more than the same, scratchy, static echoes of those fearful nights in the Quarter. The fires that sprang up had spread far and wide throughout the city, and the looting had reached fever pitch until it was finally squashed with a show of force by the military, which had now taken over the city proper. The water was rising, or it was receding, or it wasn't going anywhere. Then there was the political discourse going on. Someone had to be blamed, it seemed, and everyone was being held up to the harsh light of scrutiny one by one. All of this while it was being reported that people were still being rescued from their houses; amazing as it was to hear. We were in a period of suspended animation, each of us in our own way, for the two weeks that we stayed at my sister's home after making our escape. Over that period of time there was a lot of drinking going on, and this only exacerbated the fatigue, restless nights, and slowly fading shock. More ennui and helplessness than is advised for anyone to undergo, we received in spades. Even though things in Mandeville were seemingly coming back life to faster than expected, it was still quite hard to do anything more than get the drinks, food, ice, gas, and cigarettes you would need for the next day or so. Under the circumstances, with that many people coming and going to and from a newly occupied house I'm surprised that things weren't worse than they were. I somehow knew that there would be fallout; I just didn't have the foresight to divine when. I didn't have long to find out as it all came crashing down on our heads at exactly the worst moment of all -- hours before we were to make the next jump: the one to see Katya's family in False River.

A few days ahead of our planned exodus, my mother informed me that a family camp that we own in Bayou Liberty, La. was damaged, but not much else was known. Being that the area adjacent to it, Slidell, was decimated, we were apprehensive about what we might find should we venture out there to have a look for ourselves. I expressed reservations about the safety and timeliness of such an action, as I felt that Katya and her family had waited long enough to be reunited after their respective ordeals. I was rebuffed and marginalized by my mother, who at this point was fully gripped by the panic that had become Katrina's legacy. I clammed up, and made the run with Jason and my mother, more for the sake of the both of them than for any piece of property at the time. As was the case with any trip we made at that period, the ride there was illuminating in the darkest manner possible. Slidell and the area around it had been dealt the most physically devastating blow of the entire region that I had yet seen. Add every detail I have chronicled up until now and then smash it to tinder. It was absolute and total destruction in some areas, especially at the entrance to the old Highway 11 overpass. It's still hard to wrap my head around what it looked like, what the faces of those wandering about the destruction held with their ashen complexions and cold, dead stares.

After navigating the wreckage that was literally everywhere, we came to the small country road that led to our family camp. It was blocked by so many fallen trees that you couldn't even tell that there was a road in the first place. We gained entrance by going through a neighbor's yard due to the fact that his house and surrounding land was totally leveled . . . this didn't help our already dour attitudes in the slightest. We sloshed through the mud to find that our house, one that had withstood over 70 years of storms and age on the cusp of the bayou, had not done so well this time around. It was obviously knocked from its support beam underneath; a running water main was broken and spewing cold spring water. This had only served to erode even more of the already fragile moorings, and render the ground surrounding the house back to marshland. We couldn't gain entrance due to the shifted foundation and the swelling the house had suffered from the water so I had to break a window and climb through into the death trap my family camp had become.

The inside looked like what a house must when it is murdered. Brackish slime ran up the walls, and multicolored molds of all types covered the furniture, which looked as if it had been slam dancing right up until the point when we crashed the party. Generations of family knick-knacks were strewn everywhere and covered in foul, black ochre. It was all I could do to keep from vomiting; the smell was so overpowering. It was that of the French Quarter when I escaped; disease, festering and hungry for a new host to invade and conquer. I wrapped the handkerchief I had brought with me around my face and decided it was time for me to get out of there; such was the feeling of imminent danger. The only problem was, I couldn't go back the way I had come from and there was so much piled furniture and swollen doors blocking all of the other exits that I considered just jumping through the only window that I did have available. Of course, that would mean jumping through the glass as well. As I weighed what seemed to be my only option, Jason found a way to force a door open from the outside and we assumed the task of clearing a safe path out. Once outside and with fresh air in our lungs, Jason and I stood our ground -- we weren't re-entering that house under any circumstances. Of course in the heightened state of duress that my mother was under, she saw this as mutiny and decided that we were useless in the situation anyway. Having been freed of our responsibility, we waited for my sister to drive out and help my mother however she deemed fit. When she arrived, we sped off; shaken by the depth of damage we had just been witness to, both to the house and psychologically evident in my mother's reaction to it. The smell of organic rot and foul mildew clung to us until we arrived back in Mandeville and showered vigorously. Good thing they had multiple showers . . . I would have turned the hose on myself otherwise, as the smell was that bad.

After calming down and gathering my wits, I advised Katya and Angela that it was time to go, and no fooling around. I must have seemed a madman; I was aggressive, demanding, and curt in my instructions. They had packed while we had made our trip to Bayou Liberty, so luckily there wasn't much waiting involved. Angela was going to stay with Kelly and Trevva at their home which, as fate would have it, was just 15 minutes from my sister's home in Mandeville. We made some calls, advised all concerned that we were on our way and made hurried goodbyes considering that my distraught mother and overwhelmed sister had made it back in the time it took to gather our things and load the car with them. As we pulled away from the house, I felt a little more of the shock assert itself; it was nice to see them, and verify their safety, but they had their own trauma to work out... and we had ours. We arrived minutes later at Kelly and Trevva's house right before the horizon started to swallow the sun and walked inside to find Trevva, Kelly and Bob there. Again, sadly, the vibes were stilted, odd, and uncomfortable. They seemed as if they weren't really happy to see us, coming off more annoyed than anything else. We actually wished at that point that we could bring Angela with us on our trip but we knew that was impossible. She was so cool and calm, so pleasant to be around that we felt that maybe she wouldn't be happy there, despite just watching my aggravation with my family and the drama that entailed. We left quickly and with little fanfare, leaving behind Mandeville and its cavalcade of psychic refugees, heading for the idyllic splendor of False River.

We hit the road with our blown speakers and tinny radio blasting, the wind in our faces, and a full sense of relief spreading over us immediately. This feeling continued until we hit the outskirts of Baton Rouge to the Northwest and were hopelessly lost... again. Pull out the map, try to get the cell phone to work, go to the third gas station in a row and ask for more directions, then squabble some more. North Louisiana was harder to navigate than we had previously thought; the small towns and winding roads were all looking the same to our tired eyes. So after many calls and stops and turnarounds and arguments, Katya's brother Brian arrived at a nearby gas station to lead us the rest of the way to their False River refuge. We followed him down "Snake Road", as the locals called it, and aptly so. It was a twisting, rolling, way-too-narrow country road that fell off into steep driveways that would have bottomed out a longer car such as a Cadillac. And who would want to drive a prissy car like that out there? This was a simple town, it fostered a slow pulse, and relaxation; you could tell that they didn't lock their doors out there.

We pulled down the drive to the small camp that a kindhearted family had allowed Katya's family to use during their evacuation. You could see further beyond the house that there was a pier, surrounded by sparkling clean water. This was the Pointe Coupee', the area of the Mississippi River that had been annexed, and set up as a man-made lake. After being surrounded by the filthy water of the city during our aftermath, it was nice to see something unspoiled and pure . . . even if I wasn't going anywhere near it. There was also a swimming pool, but that first night there we were more interested in just commiserating with Katya's family and hearing their tales from the storm. We listened as her mother, father, grandmother, brother, his brother's girlfriend, and another evacuee named Chuck relayed stories of relief turned to incarceration, leaden spaghetti dinners, and local neighborhood pets needing assistance. They had held on in their house for eight days, as National Guardsmen buzzed the house in their helicopters, urging them to vacate. If it weren't for health concerns, they said they would have stayed right there, and it did seem as if they had the will to have done so.

After talking long into the night, we all made our way to sleep. I had a few moments of waking up disoriented, wondering where the hell I was, then remembering, and then going back to sleep. Over the next days we would get access to the internet, and solid land lines with generous long distance. We would also procure two new cell phones, freeing us from the confines of having to wait in line to make a call, which seemed to be happening all the time at that point. I started my long battle with FEMA there, registering online as they instructed -- only to be denied right from the start. We spent our nights eating and watching the news, which seemed to be all Katrina, all the time even that long after the storm. We New Orleanians seemed to be on everyone's lips and I have to admit, it felt good in a morbid sort of way. I felt as if, "Now they have to pay attention to us, now it's our time to get some help."

In all, it was a good week there at the house on False River. We made progress on our relief assistance to a degree, achieved communication with most of our friends and family, calmed down measurably and most importantly, all of the family we needed to see outright were verified and safe. This left us at the end of our week there feeling as if we could have stayed there a little longer, but the idea of true escape from the state altogether was so strong that it pushed us on in our quest to find our little piece of stability in all of this. We pooled our resources, advised my sister that we were returning to Mandeville for a final round of goodbyes and planning and then we were off, out there -- somewhere.

As we made our last run down "Snake Road", I wondered aloud where we would wind up, and how long it would be before we could see our home again.

Chapter Nine

September 15 - 21, 2005

– On the Road Again,
& Other Clichés –

The ride back to Mandeville was uneventful at best; we made good time and were relatively jovial through our return trip. We had learned so much about the highways and byways of the surrounding area that it really seemed like we were home in a sense, just taking a ride back from the supermarket or some such banal task. As usual, the radio gave out nonstop babble, when we could get a signal, until we started yelling at it out of anger and turned it off. Before we knew it, we were back in the blast area, felled trees and bisected houses announcing that we had arrived into the limits of Mandeville. The sun was setting by this point, so as we pulled up to my sister's home, our demeanor was quiet and reserved. We knew that our exit the week or so before was tumultuous, so we expected little fanfare upon our entrance.

As usual, my nephews responded to us as if it were any other day, making it all just a bit easier to deal with. Its funny how amidst all of the turmoil and damage, they remained so cool and collected. As we told them how much we missed them, I realized that it wasn't just the prerequisite love for a child we were expressing, we were just happy to see anyone that wasn't consumed or wrecked by the situation. I know that might sound slightly cynical and unrealistic, but at that point it was nice to step outside of it all and remember just what we had and how fortunate we were. My two nephews were the best of all possible remedies for our ailments and we enjoyed their innocence and playful natures. For the rest of my family, it was pretty much simple hellos and tired slouches. Things had not changed much since we had left, although the house and the yard were immaculate, almost no sign whatsoever of the damage that was so prevalent weeks earlier. The same went for the interior of the house; my sister had obviously been hard at work decorating her new home; trying to make it as comfortable as possible for everyone involved. We had also left the cats to stay with my family when we had left previously as it would have been too much for them to have to travel yet even more. They had been cooped up in an extra bedroom during our time in False River. We knew that they were as stir crazy as we were.

Of course, we were attacked with mewing, happy stretches, and purring; signs that my nephews had taken good care of them. As we sat and gave them some loving, we unpacked our basic belongings and decided to get to sleep early, as the next few days would be arduous; there were many phone calls to make, an itinerary to drum up, money to gather... the list went on and on and it started to dawn on us that some of the tasks we had to accomplish might not be possible in the swirling madness that was considered relief so soon after the storm in the Southern Louisiana area. I was on the phone almost daily with FEMA, pushing automated buttons and rarely speaking to a human voice that seemed to care about my plight in those first few nights of attempts. As it turned out, there was a glitch with my application, or there wasn't a glitch, no, just some crossed lines of communication . . . something was screwed, and I started to get the feeling that in the end, it was going to be me. After two or so days of frustration and busy signals, lost reception and lack of suitable lodging anywhere near our region, I was begging the Gods for some form of good news. And it came, from one of the most welcome of places. My friend James, the one who had wisely evacuated with his family after staying the night at our house, called us and said that he was okay and having a well-deserved rest in Las Vegas. His family had unfortunately suffered massive losses in the storm; his mother in particular, she lost her apartment in New Orleans East. James had gone to Las Vegas to get his head together before coming back to see if he could get back into the city and retrieve some work related documents. He also expressed a desire to see us and just be around real friends and we knew exactly how he felt. After all this time, we had not had any real tangible interaction with any of our peers -- just family and co-workers. It was like waiting for Christmas morning on the day that James was to arrive.

So when he did show up, we had to have an impromptu celebration, that much was certain. Beers, cocktails, wine, hot food and plenty of it . . . all started being gathered in the misty afternoon, one that turned to light rain and languid humidity. At one point we had staked out the front porch, shooting the breeze and drinking some cold ones, when out of nowhere we heard the loud static crack of a power transformer going out. Sure enough, it was for the neighborhood we were in. The ceiling fans went flaccid, and you could hear someone inside the house cursing. We decided to transfer some beer into a cooler should the power decide to stay out for longer than our thirsts would abide. As we sat there, we discussed the state of things, the relatives who lost everything, our feelings of being very fortunate, and the names and whereabouts of those who were still missing and unaccounted for. After a bit the lights and ceiling fans kicked on; suddenly we were fully human once more and life could resume its meaning. The best part of the entire reason for James coming down this far into Louisiana was his plan to return to the city and find out the true fate of his home and belongings. There were ways around the roadblocks and he had the credentials to work such magic if it was needed. We were invited, as it turned out, to not only go with him, but also to try and make a go at checking on our own home, verifying that it wasn't burned or looted in the aftermath of the aftermath. At that point we hadn't seen our apartment since the Tuesday after the storm and we had seriously prepared ourselves for the eventuality that we would return to either a smoking husk or squatted hovel. Here was welcome news indeed -- James arrived and had brought some sort of hope and closure to a certain part of our worries. We would know what we had, didn't have, and what we were to celebrate and mourn of our life before and after the storm.

After a bit, we all decided to get an early night in, so the next day would be as easy as humanly possible. The next morning, it was time to go and find out the truth, no matter how favorable or nasty it might turn out to be. We climbed into James' SUV and headed out towards the only working vein into the city: The Highway 11 overpass, the one that stretches over Lake Pontchartrain, was entranced by some of the worst destruction Katrina had visited. I had glimpsed a preview of the violated landscape on my way into Bayou Liberty, and now I was going to see more than I would have ever wanted to see or remember. The strangest part was that as we drove through the outlying areas, it didn't appear to be so bad from a certain point of view. It was only until we reached the promenade that the locals affectionately called "Rat's Nest Road" that our breath would catch, our gasps followed by looks of silent disbelief. It was amazing, in the worst possible way, to see what that area had suffered; this was so much, too much.

Words really do fail me at this point, but I'll try to give the best possible impression. Most stunning were the buildings, or rather the lack of buildings left. Homes and small restaurants or clubs, ones that I had been accustomed to seeing since I was a child to and from trips to Bayou Liberty, WERE GONE. No markers of their existence, not even a support beam to signal that people once lived on that spot. That is, unless you counted the pilings . . . sticking up from the marshy bayou on one side of the road and the heaps of... well, everything else, and everywhere. And I do mean everything: There were children's toys, pieces of roofing, doors, cars, machines of unrecognizable origin, furniture and business awnings strewn everywhere you looked, drywall, plumbing, and even a goddamn kitchen sink.. Most of the evidence of the crime at that point was being piled indiscriminately by the roadside in huge, dangerous heaps. As we passed slowly through a Police checkpoint at the Highway entrance, Katya snapped some shots of the more "interesting" juxtapositions Katrina had created in that area. Boats piled on top of cars on top of houses. Entire sides of apartment complexes torn off, the contents of the apartments sucked out into the parking lots, into the streets, floating in the bayou. Whole city blocks looked as if a bomb had gone off, literally. The only evidence that anything ever existed there were the huge, scattered piles of lumber, steel, and fabrics; scrambled bits and fragments, looking familiar and unfamiliar all at once.

It was actually a relief to get to the head of the line, mostly because of the looks on the faces of the people we saw whilst driving down the highway. There were relief workers and locals, military units and first responders as well as salvage companies everywhere. The look that all of them wore on their harried faces was the same I had seen days previous; dour, expressionless, graveyard stares and predominant denial displayed in downcast eyes and clenched jaws. We reached the checkpoint and were let through with no hassle; the cops were polite and efficient. We rode across the bridge in prevailing silence, digesting the damage we had just taken a tour of. We came to the area of the highway where you enter New Orleans east and got our first good look at the bathtub ring that the floodwaters had left on the buildings there. James wanted to exit to check on his mother's house, but the National Guard had barricaded the exits; the East was still off limits, it seemed. We started the approach into the nerve center of the highways, finding them deserted and so we easily sailed into town. We saw a few military vehicles coming and going, maybe one or two civilians like us, but mostly it was the creepy feeling of being the only ones around in a city that once pulsed with the souls of half a million people. We noticed the widespread roof damage to the areas just off the highway, future recipients of the blue tarps that dominated the aerial views of New Orleans and the surrounding area for too long. We finally exited near Lakeview and drove the short way to James' home in Old Metairie. Good fortune was with James, as his home was intact and showing no signs of damage whatsoever. We went inside and it was like a time capsule in there -- everything was where he left, as he left it. He even had running water and electricity. The only inconvenience other than lost time seemed to be in his refrigerator, but then very few people escaped that fate.

James grabbed essentials he had not taken before the storm, and then we were on our way into the heart of the city, to see if our fears as to the fate of our home and belongings were real. The closer we drove, the more evident it became to us that major work had been done to the city since we had escaped. Esplanade Ave. was mostly cleared of the massive trees that had fallen into the street, allowing us unfettered passage straight into the French Quarter and to our home in the Marigny. More hopeful revelations welcomed us there; our street, which had also been choked with downed trees and power lines, was immaculate and looking almost too clean considering the condition the rest of the area was in. The real capper came when we discovered that our home was still intact, within and without. After hurried scrambling through the wreck of preparations we had made in the days just after the storm, we finally found enough possessions to make the trip worthwhile in the physical sense. This made the stress level decrease yet again; our home and our city seemed relatively safe.

Leaving the French Quarter was hard, and as we drove past Molly's at the Market along Decatur Street I almost missed the short time we spent in that lawless wasteland. Almost. For its credit, the French Quarter had bounced back impressively, the streets were clean enough; and the few people we did see walking around were all pleasant and helpful. We left with a better feeling than the one we had taken with us previously, but we still wished in a way that we could have stayed; we didn't want to desert our city again, even if it didn't need us right then. As we left, we knew that it would be some time before we could come back and that thought kept us all pondering and mostly silent on the return trip. After a night of eating and drinking, James was to make his next leap in his plan; he had to work and still had family concerns to attend to. Katya and I received a much quicker answer than we expected regarding when we would see our home again. My brother-in-law told us that we could go back on the next day, as he had a work pass for the city. He would drop us off at our house, so that we could grab the last of the items that we might need in case our exile from our home turned out to be longer than expected. We accepted, resuming the farewell party for James with fervor, tipping drinks and lighting smokes into the night, his Mp3 player providing welcome music and diversion. We were so happy to have seen him again, we had missed him immensely and were happy that he was going to be okay, even if that meant we would have to miss him some more.

Next day, we said goodbye to James and then headed straight back to the city. Again, Highway 11 and the stinging dread that resided there . . . more gawking at the power and scope of the damage; something new and sad to look at every time you turned your head. Discarded fishing boats littered the highways; what became of their captains? We got back to our house and attacked it once more, only this time in reverse. We had looter-proofed it quite well actually, so we had to basically loot our own home. Of course, as we worked, those infernal helicopters were still hawking the skies, giving us shudders and fits. When Jason arrived an hour or so later, we were actually happy to go in a sense, we had forgotten how desolate and lonely our neighborhood seemed. We both held silent prayers that it would be more like we remembered it when we were finally allowed to return for good.

We made our way back to Mandeville and had the beginning of what could have passed for a normal night. A little dinner, a little more drinking and I decided it was time for me to finally start the long process of transcribing my journals onto my sister's computer. Katya and I were succumbing to the after-effects of the shock and needed a little time apart, as much as was possible in a single family dwelling. As I typed furiously inside the house, a perceived slight against me occurred outside on the patio that I, at the time, overreacted to in a most unpleasant manner. Although fuming upon my attempt to sleep, I said nothing. I was thinking that the problem wouldn't be one when I awoke, but I was wrong. The next day was one of the worst days of my life; all of the helplessness, the fear, the paranoia, and neuroses accrued in the past month or so erupted in the manifestation of a complete and total family brawl. Hard words and curses, threats and squealing tires in the driveway; crying children on a hot summer's day because the adults are acting selfish and proud -- I knew right then and there that it was time to go. The beast was there, and I had to escape it once more or else I might never learn the lesson I knew was going to reveal itself when the time was right. Somehow, a stalemate was called, and quiet uneasiness reigned over the house for the rest of the day and into the night. After begrudging acceptances and heartfelt explanations later in the evening, everyone seemed to be willing to at least tolerate everyone else and their particular problems. In light of the state of the current, we were doing amazingly well as I have noted before, but that doesn't mean that we were singing around the campfire. Katya and I renewed our pact to see each other through this game we felt we were being forced to play and decided right then and there where we were going to wind up, where we were going to find solace and sanctuary outside of the State borders. Away from the turmoil, with just enough time to get help and repair our frayed nerves.

We decided on Kansas City, Missouri. We had so many options, so many kind extensions of lodging and hospitality that it was hard to make a quick decision. After much debate and discussion, it was ascertained that K.C. would allow us to get help from Red Cross, Salvation Army, and any other agencies willing to offer relief in a timely fashion. We were told by other friends out there that the number of evacuees in K.C. was low; this meant that we would have a better chance of quick response and fewer delays in general. Also enticing was the fact that Glenn and Gill, two of the best friends either Katya or I have ever had, were already there and speaking highly of the place. Sealing the deal was that an old friend of mine, Blake, lived there and was offering to put us up until we could get a hotel room. After weighing all of the plusses and minuses, the final verdict was in: we were going straight ahead, as soon as possible. We packed through the night and prepared for a long road trip over the next two days.

Our departure the next day was thankfully quiet and unceremonious. We pulled away from the house feeling the kind of relief you might feel after quitting a job you hate, but knowing that you can always go back and see the co-workers you thought were cool. We were finally, seriously, definitely getting out of Louisiana... if only for a little while, we hoped. I assumed the mantle of navigator, cat handler, and cigarette lighter, while Katya drove us onto the highways that led away from it all. Sadly, Jack, the older of our two cats, was not having a good time with all of the moving around and intermittent incarceration. He and Loki were crammed into a small carrier for too long, for too many times in a row and he finally succumbed to the stress by simultaneously evacuating his bowels and stomach all over poor Loki and the inside of the carrier. The smell hit us like a shovel to the face and as I turned to make sure that both of the cats were going to be okay until we could stop and clean them, I saw something that still gives me the cringes.

Poor little Jack, he was mad with the heat and scrabbling at the metal grate that served as the door to the carrier. He was covered in his own waste, skittish and aggravated. Loki was behind him, yowling pitifully, as Jack proceeded to swipe at his own vomit, eating it more out of anger than anything resembling natural function. It was so sad, so disgusting, and so rank that I turned away and advised Katya to pull over as soon as possible. When we did, not only did we have to deal with two filthy cats and their rotten smells as well as the cleaning of the carrier, but it seemed that a plague of "love bugs" had descended on whatever small burg it was that we had stopped in. Swatting at the cloud of swarming black insects, we couldn't help but be amazed at the endless amount of these harmless bugs. Yet again, another seeming trait of the apocalypse was staring us in the face. We spruced up the cats as fast as possible and resumed the trek, glad to leave the smell, and the bugs, in the rearview mirror.

We drove for hours and hours after that, getting lost as usual, fighting over that as usual, all while learning more about remote areas of the country than we had ever planned on. Then another wrinkle happened that almost broke our spirits entirely. We had procured a hotel room for the night in Texarkana but something had fallen through and the room had been given to someone else. This meant that we had to find lodging somewhere else in the middle of the night, with little to no help. Frantic cell phone calls and desperate pleas for help got us a room in Little Rock, Arkansas. This was hours from our intended trajectory, but the only one available; it would have to do. We pulled in around 1:00 a.m., tired and disheveled, and bedded down in a quaint room in a small town whose name escapes me now.

The next day started early and we made haste in getting back on the road as we had lost time in dealing with the room and the concerns of the cats. We finally got back on track and as we entered Missouri proper, it finally dawned on me that we weren't in the blast zone anymore, we were just on a road trip for all intents and purposes. As we stopped for lunch in the town of Branson, I spoke for a bit with the 18 year old manager of the fast food joint we were in, and it turned out that he had relatives in New Orleans, and thankfully they were okay. After letting him in on some of the events leading us to my standing there at the counter, he told us that whatever we ordered was on him, free of charge. What a sweet kid. He would be the first in a long list of kind souls who provided relief from Katrina, no matter how small or large. As we left

Branson, the radio came alive with yet another round of dire warnings and sadness. Hurricane Rita, out in the Gulf of Mexico, was warming up for her moment in the spotlight, and was being predicted to strike in almost the same area as Katrina . . . fuck, it seemed that the Gods really did have it out for us. First came Katrina's brutal knockdown and now Rita's possible killing stroke. We knew that we could do nothing and since we were already well on our way out of the danger zone, it seemed that we had made a very fortuitous choice. A pleasant surprise was the beauty and splendor of the highway we had chosen. We were originally slated to take Route 71 into K.C., but after another missed exit we found ourselves on a smaller state road that not only cut an hour or so off of our time, but was also bucolic and filled with natural beauty. My only regret at the time was that we didn't have the camera loaded with film.

We finally pulled into the city of Kansas City at approximately 8:00 p.m., and promptly got lost some more as I listened to my friend Glenn mock us on the cell phones as we tried to find out where the hell we were. He's killer-diller. The whole time, we were impressed by the city of K.C. It reminded me of when I lived in Denver, Co. The air was clean and had a crisp bite to it that suggested that we were in a part of the country that actually experienced seasonal change. So finally, we pull up at Blake's apartment building and the smiling face of my friend Glenn Wilson. Soon after that, we were joined by Gill, Glenn's girlfriend. We unloaded the car and went upstairs to finally relax amongst friends, with no responsibilities and no expectations.

Chapter Ten

September 22 – October 7, 2005

– How to Fix a Broken Puzzle –

As my friend Glenn assisted us in prying our belongings out of the car, we felt at ease almost immediately—being around two of our favorite people ceased the angst and anxiety that had been creeping in around the edges of our thoughts. We were cracking wise and making amazingly normal conversation for the most of the night, worrying more about where the cats would be kept and where we would sleep for the next few days in Blake's bachelor pad. We loaded most of our gear in quickly, and then sat down and drank some beer while we waited for Blake to get off of work. It was good to be there; we were finally out of the clutches of the beast... or so we thought.

Glenn and Gill had escaped from the city on the Saturday before the storm, piling their menagerie of cats and dogs and belongings into Glenn's truck and heading up towards Memphis. When it became apparent that the storm was more than most locals anticipated, they then hauled themselves all the way up to Illinois, to see some family Glenn had there. After a few weeks of worrying and waiting, they both needed to find a place that would allow them to pursue their own agendas, and Kansas City turned out to be their choice. They had already availed themselves of the myriad of relief programs in town, and urged us to do likewise. We sat and traded phone numbers and sad tales of busy signals and Byzantine FEMA rituals. We watched more CNN as well; it had been almost three weeks since Katrina, and Rita looked to be ready to wipe out the rest of the coastal communities that hadn't suffered previously. Most ironic of all was the fact that Rita was supposedly hitting Texas. Actually, the storm was heading for the city of Houston, to be exact. How maddening, I thought, for all of the evacuees that had fled there—now they had to run again.

There was the issue of the already breached levees in New Orleans; there had been no time to advance any sort of repair—in fact, the floodwaters had just been pumped out of those areas. Everyone on the news programs agreed that the surge from Rita entering the Gulf of Mexico alone would flood some areas of New Orleans all over again. The only good news was that the people of southeastern Louisiana were already evacuated. As the four of us debated the impact that this second storm was going to have on the already struggling Gulf Coast region, Blake appeared, smiling and ready to have a drink or two, but only after he cleaned himself up. We kept drinking, watching our cats square off against Gill's pets, and generally just enjoying the fact that things were feeling somewhat normal. Blake showered and sat down for a bit, to ask some questions and try to relax after a long night at work. We had a few beers and shots and then we had a few more. A friend of Blake's came by, and as we started to tell our tale yet another time, he stopped us. He was also a local, and knew all he needed to know about the state of his hometown. In all, everyone seemed to be in a good mood. The weather outside was pleasant, so we decided to amble down the street to Blake's workplace, Harry's Bar & Tables. It was situated in Westport, a part of town that was packed with bars, shops, and restaurants. There were people everywhere, and it was more than a little odd, being around such a normal, unaffected environment. We went to a few other places to have more drinks, and then cut the night a little short by returning to Blake's apartment in a drunken haze.

After a hard start of a morning, I found out that sometime during our night of drinking our cats had staged a war. They had broken one of Blake's windows and it seemed that Jack, our eldest cat, had escaped. We spent the rest of the day in a sustained sense of panic, worrying about Jack and yet trying to relax as best we could. We did more storytelling, more listening, and more drinking. The situation had taken everyone involved and put them on hiatus; our lives were frozen in time, and all we could do was wonder what would become of our collective destiny. Katya and I decided that some good food would do us all well, so we rode down to the local supermarket to buy some groceries and hook up some food for Blake's outpost of evacuees. We spent the evening talking out our plans regarding all of the relief programs available in town, and it seemed that Kansas City was a good choice: Their charities were kind, generous, and as expedient as could be expected. After all was said and done, the evening was stressful, but in a strangely comfortable way—Worrying about the cat. Preparing, cooking, and serving a big enough meal to feed 5-6 people. Calling charities and organizations and family and friends. Dealing with intermittent reports on the state of New Orleans, what Rita was doing, or had done. More worrying about the cat. We had settled into a rhythm, one that was as dangerous as it was familiar. I kept reminding myself over that time that even though we were miles away from our home, and the disaster that it was, we were still there in a way.

After Blake got home from his job, we decided that another night of drinking at the local places would be a good idea, so we returned to Harry's. I drank myself into a frenzy, revisiting old demons with fervor, and making an ass of myself for the first time in Kansas City. I honestly can't say much about the next day as my previous night had left me a shambling husk of a man. About the only good news I can remember was that Jack had reappeared. It turned out that he was seeking adventure in the walls of Blake's apartment complex. He was dirty and obviously in escape mode, but after some love he calmed down and we were able to keep tabs on him until the next day. I also resumed the writing of my storm journal with the generous use of Blake's laptop computer. If there is anyone who deserves special mention for the writing of this journal, it's Blake. He allowed me boundless access to his workstation, and I made good use and quick progress as a result of his kind gesture. If you ever meet him, buy him a drink, as he would love it, and definitely deserves it.

The next day, Monday, I remember vividly. We spent that day in offices and meeting halls, sitting in chairs or on the floor. Staring into space, playing with our cell phones, and waiting for our names to be called. We finally get to speak to someone at a desk after a day of rotting in a corner, and fortune smiled upon us—we receive donations and a hotel room -- free, for two weeks. As we left the building, I was struck by the fact that we would be in Kansas City for the next two weeks, cut off from most things familiar and reaffirming. In my mind, this was where the real test was. This was where the shock would manifest; the denial, and the pain. We finally had a place that we could find out just what it was that we really needed to pay attention to in the first place. We were road-weary and disoriented, and we just wanted to have somewhere we could be alone. We wanted somewhere to work out our issues, or just let the damage continue. This was it.

Over the next week, it was pretty much a standard regimen:

Wake up from the night previous; hung-over from whatever it was we did the night before. Get a shower and get dressed. Make the applicable phone calls—family, friends, and relief organizations. Maybe play some PS2, since I had taken it on my evacuation to stave off ennui. Eat at one of the many amazing restaurants in Kansas City. (I recommend the Jerusalem Deli buffet or Pot Pie restaurant. Both kept us sufficiently full and satisfied during my stay.) Find out what everyone was doing that night, and either hanging out with them, or going out on our own adventures. Getting hammered to the point of concern, most of the time just to pass out, if not to sleep.

There were some really memorable times as well, such as the night that Blake scored the two of us a night of spinning old Punk and Hardcore tunes at a place called The Record Bar. This had actually been a personal fantasy of mine for quite some time, so it was a blast getting soused and playing some great old music with Blake, who always had the perfect song suggestion to match mine. The only complaint I have about that night was that it ended too early, but then those kinds of things always do. We also spent a good bit of time at Harry's, getting to know the staff there on a first name basis, for the most part. There were some really kind people there, and we had some great times with the fine ladies and gentlemen who work there. They were accommodating and generous, and we couldn't thank them more for their hospitality. Funny, but some people just seem like home, and the crew there did. We met Paddy O'Furniture, and Critter, Liz, and a few other guys and gals whose names escape me now. Either way, throughout our time in Kansas City, we always felt welcome there because of them, and to me, that's what counts.

After spending a week or so in Kansas City, we had a general idea where we were, and had found all of the relief centers we needed to find. This was good, as they allowed us to stay afloat and center our concern on everyone's biggest nemesis in all of this. The Federal Emergency Management Agency, more commonly known as F.E.M.A., was making everyone's life hell since the storm, including mine. I spent countless hours on the phone with their operators, haggling and harassing them at all hours of the night. Most of the time I made my calls, I was more than a little drunk, and more than a little aggravated. They had glitched my application to their website, and were moving slowly in their efforts to remedy the situation. After watching the news constantly, I knew that I wasn't alone. It seemed that while the Government's response to the hurricane was sluggish at first, it had really slowed to a crawl at this point. The constant worry over what was going to happen next was having ill effects on us, and we felt like we were in a state of suspended animation. The second week of our stay in Kansas City was clouded with more inebriants, and more withdrawal symptoms regarding our home. This was the point of the breakdown, and we felt it all come down over the next week or so. Of course, we still made it a point to hang out with Blake, Glenn, and Gill, but the wear and tear of the prolonged stress was oozing out of us at this point. We needed time all to ourselves, each one of us, so the second week was one of introspection and personal recovery. The feeling was one of settling, but not in a comfortable manner. We were sorting it all out, all of the time . . . each of us alone, even though we always had some sort of company.

There was one night, late in the second week, in which my final breakdown occurred due to the aftermath of Katrina. I had heard about some of the benefit concerts that had already happened around the country, and there was a video of some of the performances. Someone had taken footage of Neil Young playing an amazing cover of the song "Walkin' to New Orleans" and inter-cut footage of the carnage and desperation that New Orleans was experiencing. After another night of returning to our hotel room with heads full of booze, we flipped on the television to find that same video playing. It stopped everything, and froze us cold. It was so well done, and so perfectly timed, that it seemed to be a mirror of what the collective consciousness of New Orleans was thinking at that very moment -- including me. As I had before in New Iberia, I bawled like a little kid. Simple as that. The conviction that Mr. Young played his cover with was palpable, and the pictures were the ones that made the most searing impact possible. It was the final straw, and I let the feeling take over, reducing me to a sniffling mess that finally passed out in its clothes, unwilling and unable to make the requisite nightly call to FEMA.

A day or so after that, we started to plan out our next move. We had been there for approximately a week and a half, and all we really wanted to do was to go home. We had heard that the electricity in the French Quarter was back on, so we wondered if maybe our neighborhood was as well. We made more phone calls to people who were still down there, and found that while it was scheduled to come back on, our power was not on just yet. We decided to stay in Kansas City for the full two weeks that our hotel vouchers would allow, for a few different reasons. First, our home had no power, and that meant no reason to go home yet. Second, Blake was throwing a benefit for the Musician's Fund back home and of course, we had to be there. Third, was that our new friend Paddy O'Furniture told us that his birthday was the day before our hotel voucher was invalid, so we made promises to stay until then.

The benefit at The Record Bar for the New Orleans Musician's Fund was a blast. Some local Kansas City bands played, and there was some great home cooking by Blake that quickly got scarfed down. At the end of the night, Blake capped it all off by spinning a set of local New Orleans oldies. It was perfect, and we thanked him for the feeling of home, removed as it was. We capped off the night with more drinking at Harry's and a walk back to the hotel that was quiet and cold, yet soothing in the best possible way. We were only just starting to take in some of the sights the city had to offer, and now it was almost time to go. Funny, but all it seemed to take to make us feel secure and happy was the reminder of where we had come from, no matter what we had endured there.

The next days were spent packing, and fighting with FEMA as per the usual. We kept in constant contact with the people still in the city, waiting for the word that power was on, since our time in Kansas City was drawing to a close. When it came time for us to get ready to go and see our buddy Paddy O'Furniture for his birthday celebration, I made one last attempt to deal with FEMA while Katya got dressed. Amazingly, my call went through at that early of an hour, something I had not been able to do previously. I was also able to get a supervisor on the line and she had some amazingly good news—a relief check was on the way. Unfortunately, we would have to wait until it arrived at my sister's house in Mandeville, but it was still immensely welcome news that changed our outlook regarding the return trip home.

Glowing with this new development, we went out to help Paddy O'Furniture celebrate his birthday, and have one more night out on the town. We started by doing just that, bar-hopping and gathering a cadre of people who also wanted in on the party. We drank and wandered around the Westport area, and arrived at one of the most surreal and bizarre places I've ever been in my life. A Cowboy/Mexican bar, which was split down the middle, one side of the building for each cliché represented. We looked like freaks going in there, but the people there were cool, so I just enjoyed the insane juxtaposition of cultures represented.

As usual, I guess I enjoyed myself too much, because the last thing I remember about that night was being in that bar. I awoke the next morning, fully dressed and harboring that hung-over feeling that one gets when one has done something horribly wrong.

Katya was already up, and as I gauged by her reaction to me, I was right in my suspicions regarding my behavior. I had blacked out, and in a major way. I had succumbed to one of my oldest vices, alcohol, yet again. I had been using it to escape the shock this whole time, and now it seemed that I had created some of my own with my patterns of excess. As she explained what she had dealt with the night before, I felt sicker and sicker. I was a lecherous fiend, a rude bastard, and an all-around terrible boyfriend. She was pissed off and hurt, and I knew that it was really time to go. I was actually happy to leave Kansas City, not because I didn't like it, but because I felt that I had shown my ass a little too much in just a scant couple of weeks. And, I had worked through my trauma publicly, with no professional help and very little common sense. We packed our bags, corralled the cats, and loaded the car. We made a few scattered phone calls to let some people know we were coming, and some that we were going. Then we were back on the road, for one last time. We drove until the night was too deep to navigate, and then found a cheap motel room which we entered in silence and fatigue.

As we started the next day, we received a welcome call from home. The power was back on. It was time to go home. We took the quick way back, eschewing any sightseeing or breaks other than the ones necessary. We didn't even get lost -- the highways seemed to be drawing us back as if by conscious design. When we finally hit the outskirts of New Orleans, we breathed sighs of relief, despite the fact that most of the city was almost completely blacked out at that point. As we arrived at our home, we saw a few working porch lights and only a couple of people walking the street.

We pulled into the driveway, up to our abandoned little house that looked so sad and lonely. We stopped the engine and got out, amazed that from what we could see, there was still no damage; and better still, no looting. We opened the door and the smell hit us -- rot and dead air, nothing surprising. We flipped the light switches and were relived to see the lights come on. We cranked the air conditioning and started to unpack the car. We let the cats loose and as we watched them scramble playfully into their familiar stomping grounds, we knew exactly how they felt.

We were home. No matter how desecrated or disrespected it was, it was Home. And there's no substitute for that.

This Is For the City That Care Forgot

December, 2005

This is for the city that care forgot...

The city that forgot to care. This city, carelessly forgotten; our party time's behind us now, it seems. A city of ghosts, both real and imagined; all night feverish dancing to the beat of sensual drums in the virile heat. City of culinary delights, musical giants, simple pleasures and squalid splendors. A city of dust, now shrouded in mold, forever succumbing to entropic bliss on pause. This city of history, a living archive of revelry and regret. The past and the future collide in slow motion. This is the city that must be remembered and rebuilt, this bastion of visceral pleasures and historic decadence. This is for our collective delight and nagging melancholia.

This is for the ones that evacuated...

The people who left it all behind. The ones that lost almost everything, or maybe just the one thing they cared about most of all. The poor souls marooned on highways for far too long, no way home, even as the storm unleashed its initial fury. Those left deserted, no place to rest their heads, thoughts still heavy with guilt or fear or resignation. This is for the people that won't go back, can't go back, afraid of possibility and all of its attendant pitfalls. This is for those that have nothing to return to at all, not one single thing. This is for the ones that relocated, expatriates forced to strange lands with odd customs. This is for the terminally restless, the suddenly homeless, and the penniless brave.

This is for the ones that stayed...

The insane, the stranded, the curious tribes, erstwhile survivors and civic warriors alike. Those souls who stayed calm and true despite the chaos, or lost their minds to apocalyptic fancy. Battened down and hunkered low, sipping bottled water with hushed first glances, suspicious demeanors and flashlights at the ready. Proud and defiant holders of the line, sometimes criminal in intent; quick movement on the perimeters, and shoot to kill orders.

For all those who were trapped in makeshift shelters, replete with suicides, murders and rapes; victimization rank and feral. For the bitter end of salvation, acrid tastes on parched tongues dry, even as bids for escape were made.

This is for the politicians...

Federal, State and Local, at once inept and indispensable, some more than others. Caught unprepared, unconcerned, unshaven -- playing cat and mouse in a city of smoldering ruins, screams from the darkness of urgent plight, atavism gone awry. For the ignorance and obviousness, the slow motion train wreck broadcast for all to see and discuss, obfuscate and ignore. Declarations of me and mine, you and yours, pitted squarely against they and them. This is for too little, too late, the same old song played at precisely the wrong time, over and over. Nagin, Blanco, Brown, Bush, please report center stage to assume the mantle of scorn and blame -- everyone gets their turn.

This is for the ones that try to rewrite history or deny it outright, we wish we could dismiss it all so easily.

This is for the ones that died...

For the loved ones, the foolish ones, the forgotten and cumbersome alike. For the elderly, the infirmed, Vera in her cobblestone grave, the unidentified ones that received no such memorials. And our beloved household pets, loyal until the end. The parks and neighborhood greens, flora and fauna turned to sepia-tone static grey. The houses, once renowned for their architecture, are reborn as new testaments to the destructive coupling of Mother Nature and Human folly. For the spray painted X's, harsh and unrelenting, omnipresent in their emergency orange hue; 1 dog dead, 1 person saved. This is for the newest necropolis to rise, our once proud city, our interrupted way of life; breaks in the line of comfortable static. For the evidence of our empire, washed away in the eye of the storm and the turgid, toxic waters that followed.

This for the ones that rescued...

The Firefighters, EMT's, Police Officers, National Guard. To the people from far and near that just appeared out of nowhere, just wanting to help any way they could, using anything waterborne. And for the locals brave and true, risking life and limb to save just one more person, over and over and over. For all of the endless, tireless, selfless sacrifices and tear jerking humanity. For their shining light of salvation into the boundless dark, onto rooftops, inside of hacked-out attics, out of harms way to higher ground. For beaming from all directions, these beacons of hope, springing eternal and true. This is for all those who lent a hand, however small or large. Our gratitude, more than could ever be conveyed, is all we have to offer in return.

This is for the media...

The good, the bad, the ugly. For the rescuers and the soothsayers, the shelterers and the kind words. For the dispassionate, the doubters, the cynical and apathetic. The pundits and pontificators, their talking points and bad haircuts, feigning interest at all the scripted moments. For the smiles as the makeup is applied, the vacant suppression of harsh, unforgiving reality in plentiful evidence. The ones that control the present controlling the past controlled the future; as always, blissfully unaware of the consequences. For the sidebars and scrutiny, the breaking news and tight focus close-ups. Hands and mouths reacting in opposite directions, in equal amounts, all from the outside looking in. This is for the updates at every quarter of the hour.

This for the hospitals...

The nursing homes and hospices unprotected and ignored. Piling the dead or leaving them where they lay, morgues and freezers packed tight. This is for the generators that failed too quickly. No sleep or food or water or sanity or safety or hope. For our doctors and nurses, in hellish conditions, against impossible odds, this is for the ultimate and undying respect they deserve. This is for the thugs storming the gates for drugs and evil kicks on top of everything else happening, brash and ignorant of their crime.

For the hotels and hostels, kicking guests out to fend for themselves in our city gone mad. Inundation and tragedy, fragility and breakdown, the worst vacation, convention, or honeymoon ever.

This is for the looters...

For the ones that made it easier even while others made it ever harder by the minute. For the desperate, the prescient, the survivalist hordes. Scavenging and pilfering, salvaging and hoarding anything and everything of use in seemingly useless times. This is for the business owners, opening their doors wide to allow retrieval of water, food, diapers and formula, keeping their cool and doing the right thing. And for the pharmacies, their good intentions torn asunder by destructive addicts and wasteful ignorance like so many store display shelves. This is for the home invasions, the armed intrusions, for making a bad situation even worse, and for spreading the fear.

This is for the children...

The lost or outright abandoned, the marginalized or used. For the separation anxiety, trauma and tears on long hot nights that just got worse and worse. The unfamiliar and the dangerous, the abusive and profane, forsaking even common sense. For the lack of decency, for the bad examples and poor supervision. This is for the countless orphaned souls, forced to bear an adults pain with no advance warning, no preparation or guidance. This is for the countless smiles; the innocence and playfulness, the ability to make it all disappear, if only for a moment at a time. And for their will, unbreakable and resolute in its purest form and function. This is for what we owe them, first and foremost; their satisfaction will be our compensation over time.

This is for the survivors...

All of us, if any of us. Also still, the huge debt owed to those who didn't. This is for all of us in our sad, sad group, no matter where we are at the moment, home or abroad. For the hopes and dreams, reborn from the ashes of the ones previous, for our Phoenix on the bayou. For the nightmares and shock and ennui, the blank stares and paranoia deep into the night. And the helplessness -- constricting, paralyzing, and numbing. This is for finding a way to get out of bed in the morning to go to work, gut your houses and reassemble your lives. This is for those that mourn their dead, their missing, and their damaged. This is for all of us that are left to find their way back to some semblance of normalcy and well being in these dark times.

This is for the rest of our country...

Witnesses to our plight, shelters in the storm, final arbiters of our collective destiny. This is for all of the numerous benefits and donations, the concerts and the heartfelt sorrow. The letters and emails, long talks on the phone into those September nights and beyond, the shoulders to cry on and beds to sleep in. As well as the showers and food, simple things like ice and clean clothes. This is for those that are rebuilding with us, as well as for the ones that make us want to now more than ever. For the religious intolerance, the thought that somehow, we deserved this, that this was God's doing. This is for the stupidity and hypocrisy, for throwing the first stone when we were down and out. This is for their fatigue, their need to move on, not towards a better understanding, but only to the next sad refrain. For helping us stand, then forcing us to walk away stronger and more assured.

This is for the world...

The governments and their citizens, for the superpowers and third-world nations alike. For their offers and advice, their engineers and city planners, the visits of rebuilding and improved protection. This is for the feeling that we weren't alone, that this has happened before elsewhere, only much worse, and that it does get better with hard work and cooperation. For the lessons learned and experience shared; the first real promises of something good in uncertain times. This is for the most that we can share -- our lessons, our triumphs and defeats, our heartbreaks and celebrations. This is for an open welcome to the great rebuilding, our glorious comeback and their involvement in all that promises.

This is for the past...

And how not to repeat it. For the wild ride to here, the respite in its warming memories, stories and legends yet to be told. The anecdotes and folktales, the ghost stories and the pirates' songs, for history and the curious wisdom it imparts. For the good times, the bad times, the in-between times, we all had them here in this place we call home, no matter if you're local or not. This is for why we still call it home today, even if we won't, or can't be here now. This is for the sacrifices, the sweat and blood, the personal tales of reward and loss. This is for shoddy levees and interrupted communications, driverless buses and improper shelters. This is for the chance to finally get it right, to learn from our mistakes one more time, to teach others the same as well; it's that precious and rare.

This is for the future...

And the promise that it holds. For the chances in abundance, the endless, limitless boundaries presented. This is for the process of starting over, no matter how long or tough it turns out to be. For the ways to see beauty in the ugliness, to fashion something new and exciting out of something broken and in a state of disrepair. This is for our city, its legacy, our neighborhoods and families, our friends and foes alike. For our scenes and cliques, parishes and wards, businesses and hangouts, for the determination to rebuild them all. Our wishes for a better way are here and now, ready and waiting, the concept of building better, stronger and more secure. All we have to do is make it happen. This is for the here and the here from now on.

So this is for you, in your own private way. For peace, contentment, and steadfast resolve in trying times. For dignity and patience, reassuring calm after the storm. This is for the knowledge that you aren't alone, no matter how lonely it may seem right now. And for your hopeful return to the place we call home, if not now, then in due time...

For the knowledge that she will wait for you, she always has, she always will.

This is for our fair lady, our New Orleans. Past, Present, and Future.

The Lesson

August 28, 2006

– One Year Later –

Damn . . . a year. Already.

I'd say that Katrina felt like it happened yesterday, only I don't think that it has ever really stopped, at least not in the conventional sense. I guess you could argue that the enormity of the horror is over, along with the immediacy of the circumstances, but in many ways Katrina is still with us, in one way or another.

When I decided to write a coda for my storm journals, I was going to try and be clever, and wrap this diatribe up in a way that would give you the sense of what it was like to have survived the abyss that New Orleans became after the storm. I thought that it would be clever to inject some sort of mechanism into the affair, so that I might share what I have felt every day since the hurricane, and probably will for some time to come. After some consideration, I came to the idea that if I really want you, dear reader, to come to a better understanding of what a true local New Orleanian thinks and feels about all of this, that I would have to eschew any gimmicks. Ornamentation would only serve to encumber the weight of what I have to impart. Throughout my journals, I stayed true to my own idea of journalism, admittedly ripping from Dr. Hunter S. Thompson's ideas of GONZO journalism. I deliberately tried to refrain from any proselytizing or judgment, preferring to just relay what happened, and what role I and the others around me played in the proceedings. I wanted to tell the story of the average man and woman, without delving into political, religious, or sociological screeds. I feel like I delivered on that premise, especially considering that when I do get questions, it's always about what I think, who I blame, and the usual host of other queries.

So here I am, one year later, at the same time that I was scribbling in my little journal and Hurricane Katrina was beginning to destroy an entire region of the United States. Here I am, awaiting something just as potent to the psyche to arrive on our doorstep—an anniversary of violence and despair.

I figure at this point another person throwing their opinions around won't hurt; I'm really just going to do it this one time, whereas other people seem to have nothing better to do than critique and complain endlessly. I'm going to answer a few questions others have asked and offer a few words of advice from where I sit, having actually gone through the storm and the subsequent aftermath. I also hope to clear up a few misconceptions about the entire Katrina enigma in general, as even one year later those alligators are still out there biting people, if only metaphorically.

When I decided to journal throughout the storm, I had no idea that it would be the massive test of endurance that it became, although as you read through the finished work you can tell that I figured that out pretty quick. To me, it serves as an indicator of the denial that was *de rigueur* here in NOLA before the storm. One of the things that many people don't seem to understand about living in an area that is frequented by catastrophes is that you have to be able to deny that it could happen where you live. We have it down to a science here in NOLA, and still do in some ways even today. I guess another way to get a handle on the concept is to ask someone in California why THEY live there, considering that they are one earthquake away from the big swim. You do it because of familiarity, or pride, or civic responsibility. You do it for convenience, and money, or maybe for love. You do it because of laziness, or poverty, and inability. You do it because you made your choice, or because you had none anyway.

If everyone in America lived where it was "safe", we'd waste an amazing amount of space, not to mention we'd be crammed so tight we really would explode -- all over each other. We live where we live, you live where you live. Simple as that. We will move if we want to live somewhere else that offers risks more palatable. Otherwise, you're wasting your time trying to understand it, and shouldn't bother trying to wrap your head around it. And when we ask for help from the Federal Government, LEGITIMATE help, it's only because we have allowed that same Government to shaft us on so much oil money, for so long, that numbers are irrelevant at this point. If we were to be allowed a fair share of the crude oil money that is literally pouring out of the Earth, constantly, we would have a fair chance at stability and prosperity. Some estimates say that we would have enough to buy houses for thousands of homeowners soaked out of their property, and even more to help business owners reopen shuttered stores.

That's a lot of relief and restoration, folks... and then some.

See, the idea isn't that the Government hold our hands and lead us back to structure, we are too proud for that. We just need help, it's really that simple, and we just have no compunction in asking for it down here. Here in New Orleans we rely on each other in many ways that are alien, even intrusive to others, and we wouldn't enjoy our abject Bohemian lifestyles down here so much if someone didn't prop us up at some time or another. A cigarette, another cocktail, or a dinner party you just happen to crash, maybe a couple of bucks for some baby formula . . . this is a city of subtle flow and ebb, of unapologetic give and take. We didn't realize that saying that you're on the breaks is a bad thing outside of our hometown, and that makes sense considering that many New Orleanians have never even left their neighborhoods, much less crossed the state line. It's called community, and I saw just as much of that sprout up in the aftermath and beyond as I did the insanity I bore witness to. I am reminded daily that this happened to an entire region of our country, not just an area of town. ENTIRE towns are all but gone, rendered to modern day ghost facades and museums to how awe inspiring all of this really is.

I tend to think that therein might be a cause of the perceived sluggishness of recovery efforts here in Orleans Parish especially. Let's be honest here -- an entire region gets completely wiped out in a horrible storm, savagery and trauma ensues, and the Diaspora is born. Then, separation anxiety and guilt, shock and nightmares and uncertainty come and stay for far too long. Not to mention the paranoia. People in NOLA like to get passionate about issues, almost to the point of distraction, and this is the new spinning wheel -- laying the blame, and with almost surgical precision in some cases.

At this point, I'm almost certain that no matter who was in any office of any branch of Government at the time Katrina hit would have been able to do much more, or been credited with any more, at least. We need to move on from the collective guilt that we can't admit to ourselves, the guilt that none of us was prepared for this, and that we are all to blame. I can say this because it's never really happened like this before, and I never really expected it myself, although I do realize that petty mudslinging and unfounded rumor mongering is bad for the soul. So many people are hanging on to terrible thoughts, thinking that it helps them feel a little less culpable in all of this. Make no mistake, we are all to blame in this, myself included. The only thing we should be occupying our time with is better plans and projections, not pithier putdowns and escapism through spurious conjecture. That being said, I do have some thoughts to share on what I think about the most unpopular culprits in all of this, mainly at all levels of Government. To be fair, we'll start at the top and work our way down.

On the subject of the Federal Government, I really don't see how people can be so surprised by their response to this catastrophe. We are constantly shown by this administration that they are incompetent and callous to the point of cruelty. We see on a daily basis the telling evidence of their avarice and yet we acted and continue to act as if they could have done any better than they did. We are faced with the most bungling and naïve branch of Federal Government we have ever known—to me it makes perfect sense that they fouled this up so badly, and continue to do so. George Bush is an idiot man-child incapable of admitting to mistakes; he is a warmonger and Philistine -- did you think he would change when the chips were really down? Not me, I was never surprised by a thing I heard or saw from the usually indifferent right wing, or the hyperbolic ravings of the left. While they stumbled around in the dark, people died -- end of story. This is what they always do, and the only difference I see here is that there are still some people who think that a heckuva job was done, and I like to think that there is a special place for them in that Hell they believe in so intensely. The same goes for Michael Brown, for although he has been exonerated in some fashion, he was still the absolute worst man for the job. I almost start feeling sorry for him, until I think of his preening and posturing in the beginning of the aftermath. Then I realize that he was borne of the same mold that oversees those concerns, and it makes a sick kind of sense. To complain about the failures of the Federal Government in the Katrina affair is to overstate the obvious to me. Garbage sits in the White House, so naturally only garbage comes spewing out.

In the case of the State Government, the subtleties become a little more pronounced. Considering the fact that it was more fortuitous for us to have Governor Blanco instead of the previous Governor, Mike Foster, things possibly turned out infinitely better than they could have. This is considering that Mike Foster was no fan at all of New Orleans, and said so any chance he could. I feel that he was a horrible man to have as Governor, a rabid asshole outright, and an alleged supporter of that racially polarizing jackass, David Duke. That said, judging Governor Blanco by any other rubric than what she had to work with is ridiculous. Louisiana has long been marginalized on the subject of better levees, modern highways, and Federal planning regarding hurricanes. The deck was stacked against the entire state long before she was unlucky enough to get elected.

Governor Blanco, as far as I know, is not bulletproof, nor is she possessed of superhuman powers. Strangely enough, that has worked both for and against her since the storm raged into our lives. She made a major mistake when she opted to not put the screws to Mayor Nagin leading up to the storm, by not ordering a mandatory evacuation earlier. Something so simple could have facilitated efforts to coax some more people out, thus lessening the impact in human suffering and loss of life. I honestly don't think that she saw this as a Louisiana problem until afterward, when it was far too late for simple acts and words. I actually feel sorry for the poor woman, as she was off to a decent start at helping our state, and then Katrina happened. That's why I think all of the viciousness so many people have towards her is really quite silly and childish; more of that "need to blame" I spoke of earlier. Most of the ire she endures comes from her perceived skittishness when the National Guard rolled up to the city limits.

When it comes to this subject most people become Scullys and Mulders, articulating vast murderous conspiracies and pusillanimous machinations to anyone sorry enough to have to listen. The truth is far more illuminating and surprising upon simple research. It turns out that murder is the willful act of killing another person, with intent and motive, and you can't have a conspiracy unless there is at least one other person included. It's pretty obvious that Governor Blanco didn't murder anyone during the aftermath, and since there haven't been mentions of other culpable parties at the state level, that means she made her decision on her own. All by her lonesome... and how lonely it must be up there sometimes for her. As to why she asked the National Guard to hold the line for 24 hours after arriving, the crucial moment in post-Katrina decision-making happened on Sept. 2nd when Governor Blanco refused to relinquish control of the Louisiana National Guard to President Bush. This would have meant that Louisiana would have essentially been Federalized, and local and state government would have gone under the aegis of FEMA.

And we all saw how that worked out.

Honestly, I don't see how more people don't thank her for what she did, considering the circumstances. She had activated our National Guard on August 26th prior, and they were woefully understaffed already, due to deployments to Iraq and the worthless waste of time and resources that has been. Everyone begged and pleaded for more troops, and when the Federal morons finally found the time between couture discussions, they told her that she had to cede authority over the Guard, ergo the whole state procedure regarding Katrina. She said what I would have said -- Fuck that. No way was that jerk off of a President going to run this game, and stood firm. The loss of freedom and life would have been far worse in my opinion if Bush and his crew of hairless monkeys were to have taken over. And anyone who thinks that he would have not abused the precedent his takeover would have provided him, much less handed Louisiana control back so fast either, is delusional. Just ask the Iraqis about asking the

U.S. Government to leave so they can pick up the pieces. Not to mention the fact that if the Federal Government **really** wanted to help, they could have just done it, just like they did anyway, no matter what the Governor thought, and sorted everything out after the rescues and evacuations were completed. So in effect, I'd guess that criticizing Governor Blanco for her handling of the National Guard issue is a vote for the Federalization of Louisiana, and all of the sure hell that would entail. Some questions don't have any good answers; she gave the answer that was the best she could do, and saved us all from possible indignities worse that what we have endured up to now. Pretty scary when you think about it. All in all, she seems like a nice lady, but she's definitely not a career politician, and that might be the real problem in the end. She was handed the biggest natural disaster this country has seen, and unfortunately, she was far less prepared than she should have been.

And so we come to the most illustrious and notorious of our elected officials, Mayor C. Ray Nagin. Where to begin? Do I really have to at this point? Our hopelessly maverick figurehead is simply what he is, and I hope that I don't have to explain the myriad of controversial, inspiring, and hilarious sound bites he has issued in the year since the storm. He is quintessentially New Orleans—brash, indecipherably enigmatic, and more than a little rough around the edges. To be fair to the man, it's hard to tell if he actually made more mistakes, or if he just needs to stay away from cameras. He has a major problem with not being very tolerant of perceived slights against him and his city, and a sad penchant for thinking he is more eloquent than he actually is. Mayor Nagin did make some very ill-advised decisions before the storm, ones that might have helped to alleviate some of the after-effects, but nowhere near all of the problems we faced in the aftermath. Again, I feel that his was the same problem as Governor Blanco: inexperience. Neither of them was a career politician, and even though that doesn't guarantee that the Federal response would have been any different, it still implies that they didn't have the foresight to prepare for the enormity of something like Katrina. I will say that during those nights spent in that hellish sweat box in the French Quarter, we were kept a little saner by the sound of Mayor Nagin's voice, echoing the same dire concerns that we had at the time. I heard the voice of a fellow New Orleanian, the voice of a man who was admitting that this was bigger than anyone could have planned for, and that we needed so much help yet were getting so little. I heard the voice of a man who was as overwhelmed as anyone else was at the time. No one man could have surmounted the challenges presented in that time, and I defy any one man to tell me they could, or that they can name someone who could have done what most people suggest the Mayor have done. Mayor Nagin is just another casualty of the storm, admittedly sometimes by his own design, but to rob him of his humanity in all of this is downright cruel. Yes, he is not perfect, but when all is said and done, I will prefer a novice politician over a career politician any day. We've found out what the latter can do with disaster relief, right?

Whatever the cases may be with the respective branches of Government, it all adds up to one insoluble fact—no one really expected this to happen. And there we have the most lasting and potent aspect of Hurricane Katrina and also the most damning evidence. See, we are all to blame. As I have already stated, each and every one of us shoulders a bit of the blame if any of us do. We never took enough action, never demanded more levee protection, and never held anyone accountable until it was already too late. When it comes to the subject of who did what to whom and how and why and where and for how long, I just shake my head and wonder why people don't cut the bullshit. We need to collectively realize that we will only have a better New Orleans when WE make it happen. The only problem with that idea is that we all seem to think that it's the Mayor's, or the Governor's, or the President's job. It's not. So the next time you ask me what I think of the latest mini-scandal involving some momentary lapse of reason, don't be surprised when I ask you why you are missing the point entirely.

Another round of questions I get is specifically related to my journals themselves, mostly about pertinent details I might have omitted or changes that were made in editing them. There aren't many, but I feel like now is a good time to catch up to now by putting the final word on the perceived holes in the story. For example, I've been told that my perception of some of the events has not withstood scrutiny in the year since the storm and at first glance, this allegation may be true. I tried to stay as lucid as I could during the writing and editing of the journals, so as to retain the *feeling* of the events as they happened, as well as the overwhelming sense of trying to disseminate all of the information we were being bombarded with during that time. I know that to some people, things weren't as bad as I put them on paper, but really, how much is enough? I know that there weren't hundreds of rapes, but how many rapes are too many? To put it another way: when there is a commercial that features Charmaine Neville talking about her rape candidly and offering help to all of the people who didn't even report it, there were enough rapes in my eyes at least. The same could be said for the looting, which was happening everywhere I looked in the aftermath. After we came back into the city in those first weeks after the storm, we saw more than enough stores that were viciously cleaned out, with smashed windows and doors hanging on their hinges. How much is enough? The vain attempt to revise

.y only works on those fortunate to have not learned its lesson firsthand. It may sound cliché, but I was there, I saw what I saw, and trusted those that related stories that were too real to be lies or rumors. So let's be honest—there were rapes, murders, looting, and overwhelming desperation and danger during those first weeks after Katrina, more than there should be at any time. So I ask again -- how much is enough?

Now, for those that have read my journals up until now, some have noticed that I have omitted the names and locations of some of the more intense people I encountered during my ride. This has nothing to do with any type of capitulation, or act of kindness on my part, and is quite to the contrary. I simply realized that I was inadvertently giving free advertising to people that didn't deserve to see their fetid names in print. I know too well that bad publicity is the best kind, and since they know who they are, that editing works just fine with me. So from here on out, you'll have to guess who the offending parties are, and offensive they remain to this day. They're the kind of shit that makes this city harder to get along in, if only because they were, and still are, just tourists who overstayed their welcomes in the first place.

Many people have remarked that they didn't see what the point was in including my travels after I escaped the French Quarter, saying that the real story was the storm and the immediate aftermath. And while I agree that the "meat" of the story is in those passages, I guess I just wanted to show that the effects of this storm weren't over when you escaped. It followed us across the country, as my journals attest. It never really stopped in reality, as even as I write this people are in a mild state of apprehension over a simple tropical storm out in the waters off of Cuba. In the end, I like to think that I achieved what was assigned to me by the abyss. I wanted to leave a document behind that would allow people to see what everyday New Orleanians went through concerning Katrina. To me, the story really began once you left the city, regardless of if you rode out the storm or not. I wish I could print the volumes of incredible tales I have heard regarding every possible facet of my friends own Katrina experiences. Needless to say, my story is not rare, as many people I know tell similar derivations on that same theme—loss, anger, madness, folly, and uncertainty. I just wanted to document what I felt might be a really important story . . . and I guess in that one thing I was right.

One of the main issues I am asked about concerns the state of race relations in the city during the time of the aftermath. In some ways I was on the front lines, as the French Quarter became the conduit you had to pass through in your search for a way out of the water, disease, and fire.

I saw people breaking down physically and emotionally, as well as spiritually. There was an amazing amount of apocalyptic thought happening, and you could literally feel the situation getting worse by the hour over those four days. I saw more than a few poor souls completely give in to madness, unless they were drinking and drugging themselves half into a coma. I witnessed essentially good people reduced to erstwhile warriors, scared little children with guns and tough looks. I watched people take as much as they could, as some gave as much as they could afford. I saw the studied looks we received when we lit up a cigarette or drank water on those blasted streets in those initial days after the storm. Not once did I get the feeling that any of the action was based on racial concerns. People of all types and shades were just as nice to us as others were horrible to us. We were all well and proper fucked when it all went down, we were all rendered in the same bruised shade of grey. It is impossible to relate in words how much of a frontier mentality prevailed at that point; it was strangely exciting, if only for the endless possibilities at hand. Only those who went through it can understand what went on down here. In some ways we have never left; we are still in the aftermath.

What most people seemingly fail to realize is that this is just that big, the kind of big that is incalculable, and deserves to be. No one person can wrap their head around this idea, as the logistics and politics are immense and resolute. I personally think that the best thing for New Orleans would be to appoint a commission that would handle the most important aspects of consolidating immediate concerns, although the grass roots efforts down here are at times encouraging. The power is, in a backwards way, back in the hands of the people, and success really just depends on how inventive and opportunistic you are. This leveling of the field has rendered in fine detail the problems we have faced as a city since way before the storm, and while some are being repaired, others are left to fester. The one sure thing about all of this is that it has enabled us to look with clear eyes at the problems we have here in NOLA, and maybe make it better... although some things have only gotten worse. Infighting and petty squabbling has rendered certain parts of the situation hard to deal with in the extreme.

We still haven't gotten the majority of the relief money that the Feds have promised us. This leaves many in our city and state governments with the appearance of impotency, to their detriment. Luckily, public opinion of the Federal Government is at an all time low as well, so it looks like there's more than enough reality to share. In the end though, their inability to help their own citizens out during the worst disaster we've ever faced has left New Orleans prey to many forms of predators. The insurance companies are reneging on their policies, or paying out base minimums, leaving people with no clear way to rebuild their homes. FEMA releases arcane maps, with Byzantine number combinations related to the raising of homes that can't even begin to remediate yet. That is unless you live in one of their trailers, unless they still haven't given you your keys to open the door in order to allow utilities to be attached, much less turned on. The power companies are opting to hand their losses to the consumers outright, in return for intermittent electricity and incompetent customer service, all in an effort to please their stock holders. And landlords, the rankest creatures in all of the post-Katrina landscape, are choking the life out of the working-class, sometimes tripling rents in the space of a month. The excuses being that since insurance and taxes have gone up, so must the rents. These bastards must think that we are all as dumb as the day we were born, because those figures don't amount to doubling or tripling rents! This isn't to say that ALL landlords down here are greedy pigs, but enough of them are at the trough that it has caused a major problem here in NOLA. If a person can't afford to live in their city, how are they supposed to help it recover? I honestly had a realty agent tell me that we should institute a "Katrina tax" on people HERE IN THE CITY; because, you know… it's only right. She had no answer when I asked her what that would mean for people like me, who work paycheck to paycheck. It is this inability to understand another person's position that is proving to be the real problem here, as it is manifesting all around us.

People I know that love this city, people like me that want to stay, are feeling the pinch of the pocket -- many of them speak of wanting to do more, even as they are looking elsewhere in case we get priced out of town. Most folks just don't understand that the class division that was so serious here before the storm has only intensified; creating a rift that threatens the entire city. There are very few areas of middle-class prosperity here in the city, and it has created a fixed state of uncertainty that is hard to deal with in the least. But then that's really what it is all about in the end... unless you were here, or are from here, you couldn't possibly understand what it's like. When I visit Lakeview where I grew up, and see the ghost town that it has become, much less the East, or the Lower Ninth Ward, I know that the difference between perception and reality is as big as the sky and beyond. The most depressing thing overall is the sense of defeat I see in a lot of people I speak to—they are accepting the way things are now, and that is a bad direction to go in. It's almost as if we are so tired, so beaten, that we just want some kind of system, even if it isn't the one we want. But isn't that what got us into this situation in the first place?

So after all of this discourse, I feel I must answer the main question I am asked, and the one answer that eluded me, until I really asked it of myself:

What *was* the lesson, what *did* Katrina teach you?

And in the end, I guess that what I learned was that we are far more resilient than we thought, we New Orleanians. We **are** genuinely interested in rebuilding our city; we just need to quit paying attention to the momentary issues and stick to the bigger plan, the one that befits the memory of what came before. To me, New Orleans has always been about an **idea** more than just another city. There is so much history here, so much culture, and so many contributions to the world have been made in our name that it seems disrespectful to let simple problems complicate such a huge undertaking. We have to replace and rebuild an entire city, an entire region -- time is of the essence, and it never waits. If we could only find that way to put all of the petty differences aside, we could provide one of the most important and enduring lessons for the entire world. We could be a good example, the one that is held up in reference to the other problems we are sure to face as a nation and planet. We could show them all, teach them how to recover and plan better. We just need to do it, and it really is that simple in the end. All it really takes is for everyone to do their parts—Get a job, rent and buy from locals who deserve it, help others who are having trouble filing for aid with whatever resources you have, volunteer at a shelter if you can, if you're creative—create, put some sorely needed culture back, donate goods and services in some way or another, don't buy into the silly diversions and bellyaching. . . just do something, anything that actually helps, and don't ask for anything in return.

That's the lesson: to be selfless in the face of something so much bigger than you, and be happy for whatever positive role you happen to be able to play in it. And when all is said and done, that's reward enough for me.

NOTES AND EPHEMERA

FROM CNN INTERVIEW: DAVID MATTINGLY, CNN CORRESPONDENT, NEW ORLEANS: as the engine that drives New Orleans tourism, dire predictions of 20-foot flood waters in the French Quarter spelled a disaster that would have been felt for decades. But as Katrina departed, the storm instead left behind an endless parade of debris - and surprises. What's most amazing to me as you walk around the Quarter is how many people you see out on the streets right now. People who were told to evacuate didn't. The streets that could have been hit by catastrophic flooding weren't.

MIKE BEVIS, FRENCH QUARTER RESIDENT: All of these lights right here, the glass has been smashing against the wall and then coming down the street and everything.

MATTINGLY: Mike Bevis and Katya Becnel felt their century-old apartment building was up to the challenge. They made it through with just some damage to the kitchen ceiling.

BEVIS: These buildings down here, they've been here for so long, and the way they were built, that some of them, they're as tough as a bank vault, really.

RICK EICHMAN, FRENCH QUARTER RESIDENT: The wind was rolling in this way...

MATTINGLY: Upstairs, Mardi Gras bead makers Rick and Laurie Eichman stayed, so they could get an early jump on cleanup.

EICHMAN: French Quarter residents are pretty hardy types. We're ready to start cleaning up and getting the show back on the road. And we want to have the place decent by Labor Day, so everybody can come down and have a good time.

MATTINGLY: It may be an ambitious goal.

Local residents became sightseers themselves, so they could take in all the damage. There's one thing down this street that all the residents tell us we have to look at, and it has nothing to do with all of this debris in the street. It's right around this corner. In this park, we can see some huge trees that are down, crashing through the gate over here. But it isn't the trees that they wanted us to come look at. It's what's inside. Massive oaks fell all around, but not on, the statue of Jesus. The only apparent damage to the church -- a clock that stopped when electricity failed. And even as the rains from a receding Katrina continue to pour, there were signs the party was coming back to life.

From Klaus Marre's German News Agency article:

Law of the jungle governs in New Orleans. In the roads naked force prevails in the Jazz metropolis -- Plundered gangs pull by the city. Hunger and greed are everywhere in the city. The force escalates again and again.

By <u>Klaus Marre</u>: New Orleans. Humans in the once magnificent port New Orleans are, after the tide, only a shade of their former humanity. The relaxed kind of the inhabitants changed fundamentally. In order to survive the city or be able to leave in the chaos, they forget law and conscience. From the famous "Big Easy" to the city is nothing more to be felt. New Orleans sinks after "Katrina" not only in the water, but also in the anarchy.

"They are no longer humans", said <u>Michael Bevis</u>. As most people staying in New Orleans can tell frightening stories of murders, rapes and plundering. Humans became ever more inconsiderate -- it was from hunger, guilty knowledge, lacking, or pure greed. Plundering from supermarkets are the agenda, meanwhile the police tolerate even the theft of food or other vital goods, according to observers. But the robbers want more; leaving the businesses with trolleys full of clothes, for example. The force in shootings between law crushers and policemen escalates again and again. Humans are shaken also by reports by the rape of a 13 year old girl in the Convention center. A woman told, both foot joints had been broken on the girl. "We went to us to the police and were told to stay there; we had been supposed to leave the city before the storm -- now we would have to live thereby".

The Governor of Louisiana, Kathleen Blanco, requested 40,000 National Guardsmen, in order to provide for order. President George W. Bush announced "zero tolerance", opposing plunderers. But there are indications of humanity, also encouraging. In order to protect themselves against criminals, groups divide their meager meals and stores of water. "There is no assistance otherwise", says John Fulton, who was stranded as a tourist in New Orleans.

From www.lowerdecatur.com:

MySpace users reprint their Katrina related journals

Many users of the insanely popular online social networking site MySpace.com have recently, in recognition of the anniversary of Hurricane Katrina, posted reprints of their evacuation from and return to New Orleans journals. A couple of the better ones that mention spots on Lower Decatur Street area are listed below.

The one who calls himself M. Bevis writes this tale.

"As we made the approach to Coop's, we noticed that Molly's at the Market was open. This was a popular bar amongst the hip underground set, so it made us feel a little at ease to see that they were at work. We spoke with Jim Monaghan Jr., the owner of Molly's; he told us that Coop's was talking about preparing the food, but with the water being out, it was not looking good. He told us there were cigarettes and beer for sale in his bar and that we were welcome as long as Molly's was open. One of Jim's friends made a joke after I thanked him for his generosity and sanity that that might be the first time anyone has said anything like that to him. I don't care. Either way, I meant it then, even more so now."

About the Author:

M. Bevis is a New Orleans native, with over five generations of his family hailing from the Louisiana region. He was raised in the Lakeview area of NOLA, although he has lived in almost every parish of the Greater New Orleans area at one time or another.

He has been a local artist, musician and writer for over twenty years, and performed with his experimental music group Gimp, from 1991 to 2003. His current musical project is titled Star of Kaos. He is a frequent contributor to PARANOIZE magazine, a free local paper that celebrates the New Orleans Underground music scene.

M. Bevis has not left New Orleans since returning from his evacuation. He lives in the Marigny with his partner Katya, who provided the photos for the book, and their two cats Jack and Loki, who also rode out the storm with them. As of this writing, their family and friends are all well, and both of their families have returned to their homes in Lakeview and Broadmoor, which were almost destroyed by Hurricane Katrina.

This is the first published work by M. Bevis, and he hopes to never have to write about such subjects again... not in this lifetime, at least.

Printed in the United States
203388BV00002B/340-345/A